Device Fonts

Ten Year Itch | Rian Hughes

Miserichordia Regular 60 and 29pt

Other books by Rian Hughes

The Science Service
{with John Freeman}
Magic Strip/Acme, 1989

Dare
{with Grant Morrison}
Fleetway Xpresso, 1992

Firewords
{with John Foster}
Oxford University Press, 1999

Art, Commercial
Die Gestalten Verlag, 2001

In preperation:
Eau de Nile, Cream and Oxblood
Palmano Bennet, 2006

Rian's typefaces are unique because he is unique — a type designer that can actually draw, a fundamental skill for creating well proportioned, properly crafted characters and typefaces. His work often has a sense of fun, too. It celebrates the joy and dynamism of life, a very good reminder for those in typography who forget that letterforms should express the whole range of human emotion and not merely be 'serious'. Fun, serious: either way, Rian always produces fonts with an expertise and commitment that gives his work great depth.
Jonathan Barnbrook

Rian Hughes is brit-pop for typography at its best.
signalgrau.com

Try a death tango in the upper levels of the stratosphere with smoke Cyrillic logos wrapped around your fuselage and raw Letraset moiré crackling away in the rearview and then maybe you'll earn my respect the way Rian Hughes earned my respect long ago.
Grant Morrison

Chances are you've seen his work somewhere if you're at all plugged into pop culture… dazzling, rife with style and energy.
Buddy Jarjoura, YPP.com

Rian Hughes, the influential designer.
The Guardian

It's undeniable Rian knows how to design type. The concepts he comes up with are well-fleshed out and impeccably executed, resulting in balanced, coherent typefaces. He manages to inject a unique personality into each of his designs and — what's even more important — succeeds in keeping it up throughout the complete character set.
Yves Peters, www.typographer.org

Hughes' style is both distinctive and unique. Unalloyed delight.
m-web.co.uk

Device Fonts:
Ten Year Itch 1995-2005 [Extended European Remix]

Call us! Device provides graphic design, logo design, type design,
illustration and art direction for a wide range of clients in
music, fashion, comic books, corporate, TV, film and publishing.
A web portfolio can be viewed at www.devicefonts.co.uk.
Telephone: (UK) 0208 896 0626. rian@rianhughes.com.
Device: 2 Blake Mews, Kew, TW9 3QA, UK.
Join the Device forum: http://devicefonts.co.uk/forum/

Thanks to Veen, FontShop, FontWorks and t-26.

Limited edition hardback: ISBN 0-9551376-1-6
Paperback: ISBN 0-9551376-0-8

Printed in China. Expanded 2nd edition: 2005. 5 4 3 2 1

We are always interested in seeing Device fonts in use. Please
send or email us examples. These may be featured in a
future publication; full credit will be given.

A special tip of the circumflex hat to Colin Brignall, designer
of Countdown and numerous other Letraset faces that
provided early inspiration for this future typographer

Most fonts contain the following characters:

#1234567890ªº£€$¢ƒ¥x+÷–=←→%‰%₀AÆÄÅÃÄÅB
CÇDÐEÈÉÊËFGHIÍĨİJKLŁMNÑOŒØÒÓÔÕÖPÞQRSŠTU
ÙÚÛÜVWXYÝŸZŽaæàâäãåābcçddeèéêëāffiigghiíĩıjklłm
nñoœøòóôõöppqrsßštuùúûüvwxyÿğgzž@®©®&!!?¿«
»0●™*ʰᵗᵐᵘ„"°ˇˆˉˇ´ˋ˝¯~¨˜···;,:.·_[]()[]_ʌↆↇↈ~-–—

All fonts have been updated to contain the Euro symbol '€'
in the alt-2 character slot. Selected fonts also contain
fractions and superior/inferior numerals. Please ask for
details.

For music industry use, a publishing 'Ⓟ' is available in the
alt-p character slot in all fonts.

These days, everybody now knows what a "font" is (and it's not the same as a typeface, by the way). If only people knew that, while type design may result in a product for creative use, the actual process of drawing 255 glyphs tends to involve a lot of tedious copy-and-pasting, meticulous attention to detail and altogether a lot of patience. Remember that a normal family of typefaces needs at least 4 members plus extra characters, dingbats et al, and you're faced with having to draw a few thousand of them.

Rian Hughes also has to generate 255 glyphs per font, but for some reason he has managed to escape the seemingly inevitable fate of becoming a boring old type designer. Partly, of course, this is due to the fact that he has (so far) avoided producing a family of text faces with 144 weights; the other answer could be that his head is constantly full of so many of these weird characters, signs and images that drawing them onto a screen serves as a therapeutic measure. Or maybe Rian has never grown up and still thinks that connecting dots on screen is like one big video game.

Whatever the amateur psychologist may say: Rian's typefaces, comics and publications are anything but boring. When I first discovered his fonts about twelve years ago, I was simply struck by his talent: whatever he touches turns out to be funny, cool and amazingly functional. In his case I have to say: More is better. Keep it coming.

Erik Spiekermann

DF Paralucent → Full family listing page 129 | DF Yolanda → Full family listing page 86

FontFonts
Released 1994-1995

FF Crash Bang Wallop ©1987/93
FF Identification ©1993
FF Knobcheese ©1992
FF Outlander ©1993/5
FF Revolver ©1990/1992
FF Rian's Dingbats ©1993
FF TypeFace ©1993

Device Fonts founded 1995

Device Collection 1
The first 100
Released 1997

DF Amorpheus ©1995
DF Autofont ©1997
DF Bingo ©1997
DF Blackcurrant ©1997
DF Bordello ©1997
DF Contour ©1992
DF Cottingley ©1993
DF Cyberdelic! ©1993
DF Darkside ©1992
DF Elektron ©1992
DF Foonky ©1995
DF Griffin ©1997
DF Judgement A ©1995/6
DF Judgement B ©1995/6
DF Judgement C ©1995/6
DF Lusta ©1995
DF Mac Dings ©1994
DF Mastertext ©1994
DF Metropol Noir ©1996
DF Motorcity ©1997
DF Pic Format ©1995/7
DF Quagmire A ©1997
DF Reasonist ©1992
DF Regulator A ©1993/7
DF Regulator B ©1993/7
DF Ritafurey ©1992/6
DF Scrotnig ©1993/7
DF Stadia ©1996
DF Telecast ©1996
DF Transmat [Transit] ©1995
DF Untitled 1 ©1994

Device Collection 2
Coachhouse Garage
Released 1999

DF Ainsdale ©1992
DF Anytime Now ©1997
DF Chascarillo ©1990/1994
DF Doom Platoon ©1997
DF English Grotesque ©1998
DF Gargoyle ©1998
DF Gran Turismo ©1998
DF Gran Turismo Ext. ©1998
DF Hounslow ©1998
DF Jemima ©1993
DF Laydeez Nite ©1997
DF MenSwear ©1998
DF Quagmire B ©1998
DF Quagmire Extended ©1997
DF Silesia ©1998
DF Slack Casual ©1998
DF Space Cadet ©1993
DF Terrazzo ©1997
DF Wexford Oakley ©1997

Device Collection 3
Salem
Released 2000

DF Blackcurrant Alts. ©1999
DF Bullroller ©1999
DF Citrus ©1999
DF GameOver ©1999
DF Vertex ©1999
DF WhyTwoKay ©1999

Device Collection 4
Moscow Low
Released 2001

DF Acton ©1998
DF Haulage Commercial ©2000
DF Jakita Wide ©2000
DF Mystique ©2000
DF Novak ©1999/01
DF Paralucent ©2000/01
DF Range ©2000
DF Register ©2000
DF Register Condensed ©2001
DF Register Wide ©2000
DF Sinclair ©1998
DF Skylab ©2000
DF Zinger ©2000

Device Collection 5
Under the Westway
Released 2002

DF Data 90 ©2002
DF Flak ©2002
DF Flak Heavy ©2002
DF Freeman ©2001
DF Iconics ©2002
DF Paralucent Cond. ©2001/2
DF Paralucent Cond. It. ©2001/2
DF Paralucent Italic ©2000/2
DF Platinum ©2002
DF September ©2001
DF Substation ©2002
DF Westway ©2002

DF HotRod ©2002
(available only with "Art,
Commercial" retrospective)

Device Collection 6
The Common Room
Released 2003

DF Cantaloupe ©1998/03
DF Cordite ©2002
DF Gravel ©2003
DF Klaxon ©2003
DF Mercano Empire ©2003
DF Mercano Empire Cond. ©2003
DF Mercano Empire Lined ©2003
DF Paralucent Stencil ©2003
DF Popgod ©2003

Device Collection 7
Pagodaland
Released 2004

DF Absinthe ©2004
DF Chantal ©1993
DF Dauphine ©2004
DF Drexler ©1994
DF Dynasty A ©1998/04
DF Dynasty B ©1998/04
DF Egret ©2003
DF Electrasonic ©2004
DF Galaxie ©1992
DF Galicia ©2004
DF Glitterati ©2004
DF Gusto ©2003
DF Interceptor ©2004
DF Miserichordia ©2004
DF Monitor ©1998
DF Moonstone ©2004
DF Outlander Nova ©1993/04
DF Payload ©2004
DF Pitshanger ©2004
DF Radiogram ©2004
DF Ritafurey A [extension] ©2004
DF Ritafurey B [extension] ©2004
DF Rogue Sans ©2004
DF Rogue Sans Cond. ©2004
DF Rogue Sans Ext. ©2004
DF Rogue Serif ©2004
DF September [extension] ©2003
DF Sparrowhawk ©2004
DF Straker ©1997/04
DF Telstan ©2004
DF Xenotype ©2004
DF Yolanda ©2004

Device Collection 8
Zephyrmen
Released 2005

DF Box Office ©2005
DF Catseye ©2005
DF Catseye Narrow ©2005
DF Custard ©2005
DF Gentry ©2005
DF Gridlocker ©2004
DF Ministry A ©2005
DF Ministry B ©2005
DF Mulgrave ©2005
DF Payload Narrow ©2004/5
DF Payload Wide ©2004/5
DF Roadkill ©2005
DF Valise Montréal ©1989/2005
DF Yellow Perforated ©2005
DF Zond Diktat ©2005

Ten years. 400-plus fonts. Four studio moves. From Ealing Studios to Salem Road, Bayswater, to the shadow of the Trellick Tower (where a fellow Westbourne Studios member had a gun pulled on him) to close by Kew Gardens' Pagoda (where, if you're really unlucky, you might have a cucumber sandwich pulled on you).

This anniversary suggested a small celebration was in order, and that the time was right to make some space in the schedule to finalise new designs, embark on some fresh experiments and to trawl the archives for forgotten gems. This new catalogue is the most extensive yet, showcasing over 100 new designs and several extensions to popular existing families.

This project has also proven to be something of an archeological dig. There are fonts here that were started in 1993 when Altsys Fontographer was still fresh out of the box: two years before Device Fonts was founded, and four years before the range was launched with the first 100 designs in 1997. **Galaxie** and **Dynasty** (to pick a couple of random examples) by rights should now have been commercially available for a decade, but somehow managed to slip out of sight and out of mind as other projects came to the fore. They are contemporaries of the first FontFont releases, but apart from occasional use on studio work are available here commercially for the first time. Others have been awaiting the addition of full international character sets: *CHANTAL*, for example, was designed to letter the RoboHunter series that Peter Hogan and I produced for 2000AD in 1993. At the time it famously elicited letters from readers who found it hard to read, but looks surprisingly friendly in its old age.

There have been unexpected hits — fonts that have shown immediate popularity and become frighteningly widespread; there have been fonts that have been slow burners, selling slowly but steadily; and there have been those that have languished at the bottom of the sales lists like John Foxx's back catalogue at Honest Jon's. Let's be generous; maybe they're waiting for prevailing tastes

to catch up with them and their time will come. Some will get picked up – **Paralucent** by Heat magazine, or **English Grotesque** by the Australian version of Harper's Bazaar, or **SCROTNIG** (Thargspeak for 'great') by MTV – and the exposure will prompt a flurry of other uses in other areas by other clients. Sometimes these "other uses" have turned out to use back-engineered illegally distributed or horribly customised versions, one of which, I was told, crashed machines and amusingly failed to print at crucial junctures, but our font police (I will have to design them a logo) have shown them the error of their ways and the pirates have invariably been made to walk the plank.

It's a simple process to licence a font for a large product launch or to allow for its inclusion in the 'bible', or even to commission a new font – something suitably fresh and unique. Custom font design has been the laboratory testing ground for some of the most popular Device designs.

These custom fonts started as projects for a broad range of advertising clients and magazines. Recently the **Rogue** family was designed as an accompaniment to **Paralucent** for Loaded, London's notorious lads-mag that had found its design being cloned by the competition and sought something unique to set it apart. The project was ultimately shelved, but now **Rogue** is here and available to all. Likewise, **Citrus** was produced for the Body Shop's 'Street Scents' campaign, and **SCROTNIG** and **JUDGEMENT** for the UK's 2000AD.

The new designs appearing here for the first time in what is the seventh and largest update so far show a spread of headline and text/headline styles. There is also one revival.

Type revivals can be less straightforward than might be imagined. For starters, many new characters and weights usually need to be designed to fill out a versatile and extensive modern family. This was certainly the case for **DF Ministry**, which features seven weights and a corresponding set of true italics.

The story behind this very English font made intriguing research. Following the Warboys Report of 1963, 'Transport Alphabet' was adopted by the Ministry of Transport for use on all British road signs. However, M.O.T. documents archived at the National Archives in Kew, England, give details of the original alphabet, still to be seen on rare surviving pre-Warboys road signs and on many street names, which were generally felt to be less important to the driving

APPENDIX VII
Diagram 2

ABCDEFGHIJ
KLMNOPQR
STUVWXYZ.
1234567890

Opposite page and this page:
Pages from M.O.T. documents
archived at the National
Archives, Kew, UK, and
contemporary photographs of
surviving street name signs.

Below:
Comparisons between the
alphabet as shown in the original
1933 guidelines [right, below] and
the revised version taken from
photographs of actual signs and
as seen in later M.O.T.
publications [left, below].

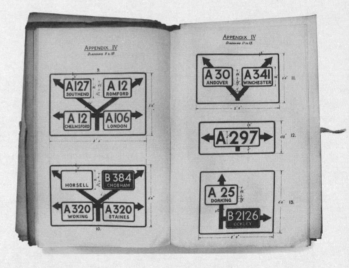

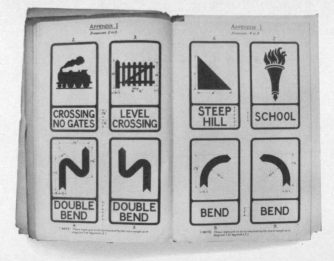

public and so were left unchanged. The medium weight of 'Minis-try' is based partly on blueprints provided in the 'Report of the Departmental Committee on Traffic Signs, HMSO 1933', and partly on the actual signs, which have been photographed around London and Bristol. Comparisons reveal that the S, G, M and K were all altered considerably in use, and all changes except those to the K were a noticeable improvement.

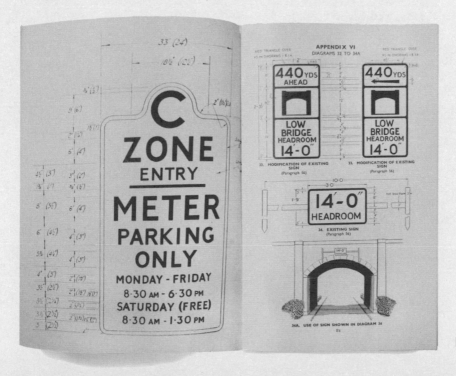

This design became known as 'M.O.T. Standard', 'M.O.T Revised' or simply 'M.O.T'. The Device digitisation uses the revised versions of the G, S and M but retains the original form of the K. These choices were made for purely aesthetic reasons.

The identity of the original designer is not preserved; however, Anthony Froshaug in his 1963 'Design' magazine article mentions Edward Johnston as an advisor. Speculation that the design was based on Edward Johnston's design for London Transport is discussed in further archived government documents from 1957: "So far as I am aware, the Ministry alphabet was not based on Johnston's design; indeed it has been suggested that Gill got his idea from Johnston. Our alphabet was based on advice from Hubert Llewellyn-Smith {then chairman of the British Institute of Industrial Art} and Mr. J. G. West, a senior architect of H. M. Office of Works" (Huddy). A hand-written addendum states "I understand that the MOT alphabet was also designed, or at least given it's final shape, by {graphic designer David} Kindersley" (Hadfield).

The original 1933 report shows only capitals and numerals, in a single weight with a slightly condensed set of alternative capitals. The lower case and the extended family of weights and italics are of entirely new design, but adhere as closely as is possible to the upper-case model. It has similarities to the later 'Series E Modified /Lowercase', the typeface used on modern American freeway signs, though there are crucial differences. The font has been produced with the permission of the National Archives, Kew.

A guided tour of the rest of the new collection begins with Box Office **PG**, designed for the 'Radio Times' film pages and extended to cover US and UK ratings plus DVD and video packaging icons. **Catseye** is a casual sans that has similarities in the curved strokes to Stephenson Blake's Grotesque series. **Custard** was designed for a children's book project that is looking for a publisher; **Gentry** is sleek cutting-edge technology for the modern executive. **GRIDLOCKER** has characters based on an isometric grid and is available in negative and positive versions.

MULGRAVE is taken from the UK's cast-iron Victorian street name signs that predate the aforementioned 1933 M.O.T. revisions. London features many different styles for these signs; they often change from district to district according to local council whim. During the second world war the right hand end was sometimes sawn off, {Aston Road, opposite} thus removing the postcode district information in a measure intended to confuse any invading Germans. **MULGRAVE** has been designed to preserve the worn and rusted quality of the originals.

A photograph taken from a flyover in Hong Kong provided the starting point for **ROADKILL.** Shaped by the width of a white brush

stroke and eroded by constant tyrewear, it's condensed aspect is due to the necessities of clarity from a low viewing angle.

Valise Montréal is a compressed brush-drawn design that can evoke feminine elegance when set letterspaced or suitably coloured, or in a seeming contradiction, rough graffiti grittiness, depending on the context. Though loose, it has even colour in longer settings. Xenotype is an examination of heavy horizontal weighting and develops ideas underlying such headline gems as 'Sintex' and Letraset's later 'Zipper' of 1970. Egret attempts to make peace between the end of the 19th century and the beginning of the 20th - ornamental modernism in two interchangeable matching fonts. ABSINTHE explores forms based on a truncated ellipse and eschews straight lines to give an entirely modern take on some of the forms more closely associated with Hector Guimard. GUSTO comes in three related variants that go from hot-dog to melted chocolate, a gastronomic combination not to be passed up (or thrown up).

PAYLOAD began as another early concept for Loaded magazine, and here is developed into a clean outline and rough splattery spraycan version. In this, the upper and lower case characters are subtly different enabling a more realistic appearance to be achieved by flipping between cases whenever characters occur together in pairs. Straker is named after the beige Nehru-collared commander in Gerry Anderson's masterpiece, UFO, and Telstar nods respectfully in the direction of Colin Brignall's 'Countdown' from 1965. Moonstone is for all those misunderstood goth Buffy fans, while Glitterati is Disko 2005; both these fonts contain alternative versions that enable customisation of headlines and are intended to be freely mixed in one setting.

Dauphine is an elegant caps and small-caps typeface that manages to be modern while still displaying perfumed good breeding, and comes with a leafy decorative variant; INTERCEPTOR should be used on cherry-red jacked up Ferraris and brainless summer blockbuster action movies. SPARROWHAWK, a capitals only titling, evokes a suburban English gentility; **Radiogram**, pure digital bakelite, can be layered – the solid variant can be placed under the striped version to create two-tone effects. **Galicia** is a looser face that has unusual forms that are seen to good effect in characters like the lower case a, and is suggested for use where a more formal and classic yet still warm and calligraphic look is appropriate. *Electrasonic* is a neon linking script in fine, X fine and XX fine weights that whispers slyly of louche backstreet glamour and medicinally strong day-glo cocktails. Use with a cosmopolitan to hand and Suede on the ipod. **drexler** is a logically constructed molecular font built via nanotechnology and mathematically derived geometric permutations. **Dynasty** is an exploration and modernisation of the typographic quirks associated with the 'American Gothic' type school (in much the same way as **English Grotesque** was an exploration of Gill/Johnston idea-space) and adds chamfered elements to dots and tails to emphasise and extend the early machine-made aesthetic.

Miserichordia evolved from photographs taken on a trip to Venice and instigated a sharp turn left into more idiosyncratic and decorative serif fonts, something of a new direction for Device. It was immediately followed by **Pitshanger**, loosely derived from a shop sign in Limoges, France, and Yolanda, a family of three weights each more florid than the last.

OUTLANDER NOVA is a reworking of **OUTLANDER**, and adds upper case characters in addition to the previously available unicase versions. This new version also provides italics for the first time. **MONITOR** is an early experiment in TV-wall pixeldom, and has the unique property of becoming easier to read the further away one gets.

Coming across a Device font far from home is an experience not unlike hearing a favourite song float out of the radio. Many users send us their samples, photos and found uses. Please feel free to continue this tradition.

Rian Hughes | Device | Kew Gardens, UK | 2005

New Fonts

Miserichordia Regular 60pt

PRAGUE

Absinthe Regular 202pt

EXPERIENCE ALTERATIONS IN CONSCIOUSNESS, AUDITORY AND VISUAL HALLUCINATIONS.

Absinthe Regular 18pt

MILKY GREENISH-WHITE

Absinthe Regular 65pt

DR. ORDINAIRE

Absinthe Regular 105pt

ARTEMISIA ABSINTHIA

Absinthe Regular 71pt

LOUCHE

Absinthe Regular 201pt

Box Office 24pt

Box Office 30pt

Box Office 44pt

Box Office 196pt

Gridlocker Two 53pt

Gridlocker One 42pt

Gridlocker Two 124pt

Gridlocker One and Two 37pt and 17pt

Troy Carafe

Catseye Narrow 100pt

waterproof, fogproof and shockproof

Catseye Medium Italic 22pt

The very rare Catseye gemstone is semi-transparent and exhibits a sharp white eye. The best cat's-eyes from Sri Lanka and Brazil exhibit a milk and honey effect, a secondary star phenomena, minor inclusions and sparkling transparency. By the tonne: £530.00

Catseye Medium 7pt

The very rare Catseye gemstone is semi-transparent and exhibits a sharp white eye. The best cat's-eyes from Sri Lanka and Brazil exhibit a milk and honey effect, a secondary star phenomena, minor inclusions and sparkling transparency. By the tonne: £530.00

Catseye Medium Italic 7pt

The very rare Catseye gemstone is semi-transparent and exhibits a sharp white eye. The best cat's-eyes from Sri Lanka and Brazil exhibit a milk and honey effect, a secondary star phenomena, minor inclusions and sparkling transparency. By the tonne: £530.00

Catseye Bold 7pt

The very rare Catseye gemstone is semi-transparent and exhibits a sharp white eye. The best cat's-eyes from Sri Lanka and Brazil exhibit a milk and honey effect, a secondary star phenomena, minor inclusions and sparkling transparency. By the tonne: £530.00

Catseye Bold Italic 7pt

sublime paper and ink processing

Catseye Bold 23pt

Steffi

Catseye Bold Italic 125pt

The very rare Catseye gemstone is semi-transparent and exhibits a sharp white eye. The best cat's-eyes from Sri Lanka and Brazil exhibit a milk and honey effect, a secondary star phenomena, minor inclusions and sparkling transparency. By the tonne: £530.00

Catseye Narrow 7pt

The very rare Catseye gemstone is semi-transparent and exhibits a sharp white eye. The best cat's-eyes from Sri Lanka and Brazil exhibit a milk and honey effect, a secondary star phenomena, minor inclusions and sparkling transparency. By the tonne: £530.00

Catseye Narrow Italic 7pt

LIMITED LIFETIME WARRANTY

Catseye Medium and Bold 30pt

ALIEN ENIGMA

Catseye Narrow Italic 80pt

SHOPPING LIST

- SHOWER CAP
- BARLEY SUGARS ✓
- GARIBALDI BISCUITS
- BOX OF DATES
- CORN PLASTERS
- SHERRY ✓
- STERADENT
- VIC CHEST RUB ✓
- BABYCHAM
- PARMA VIOLETS
- ECCLES CAKES ✓
- CORNED BEEF
- SPAM FRITTERS ✓
- CABBAGE ✓
- BRUSSELS SPROUTS
- 1 DOZEN EGGS
- LETTUCE ✓
- CUCUMBER
- BATTENBURG CAKE ✓
- BANANAS ✓
- HANKIES ✓
- CURLY WURLYS ✓
- FISH FINGERS
- IZAL TOILET PAPER
- FLOSS ✓
- PEOPLE'S FRIEND ✓
- FONDANT FANCIES ✓
- BLEACH ✓
- COAL TAR SOAP ✓
- COTTON BUDS
- LARGE RIZLAS ✓

Chantal Medium 15pt and 10pt

DON'T FORGET TO LEAVE THE DOOR ON THE LATCH SO THAT THE CAT CAN GET IN & OUT.

MOST IMPORTANT! PLEASE LEAVE HIM SOME WATER IN HIS LITTLE BLUE BOWL.

THANKS x

Chantal Light, Bold & Medium 23pt

STORE OPENING HOURS
MON-FRI 9.00AM-10.00PM
SATURDAY 9.00AM-7.30PM
SUNDAY 10.00AM-4.00PM

Chantal Light 12pt

STORE OPENING HOURS
MON-FRI 9.00AM-10.00PM
SATURDAY 9.00AM-7.30PM
SUNDAY 10.00AM-4.00PM

Chantal Medium 12pt

STORE OPENING HOURS
MON-FRI 9.00AM-10.00PM
SATURDAY 9.00AM-7.30PM
SUNDAY 10.00AM-4.00PM

Chantal Bold 12pt

STORE OPENING HOURS
MON-FRI 9.00AM-10.00PM
SATURDAY 9.00AM-7.30PM
SUNDAY 10.00AM-4.00PM

Chantal Light Italic 12pt

STORE OPENING HOURS
MON-FRI 9.00AM-10.00PM
SATURDAY 9.00AM-7.30PM
SUNDAY 10.00AM-4.00PM

Chantal Medium Italic 12pt

STORE OPENING HOURS
MON-FRI 9.00AM-10.00PM
SATURDAY 9.00AM-7.30PM
SUNDAY 10.00AM-4.00PM

Chantal Bold Italic 12pt

Rhubarb Crumble

Custard 37pt

Join Jolly Rodger and his seaside chums for a holiday celebration of titanic proportions! PREVIEW TICKETS ON SALE FROM TODAY

Custard 37pt

Oasis
Bikini Pool Party

Custard 185 and Custard Condensed 76pt

San Diego "Some like it Hot" Hotel del Coronado

Custard Condensed 26pt

Feeble Fitzsimmonds and Wishy-washy Wilf... together again in their first full-length animated movie! Certificate 18

Custard Condensed 18pt

Feeble Fitzsimmonds and Wishy-washy Wilf... together again in their first full-length animated movie! Certificate 18

Custard 18pt

GRUMBLE MUTTER GRIPE

Custard 36pt

PHUNKSHUNAL

Custard Condensed 83pt

ESSENTIAL TO THE THEN DEVELOPING COLONIES, KEW GARDENS SUPPLIED THE EMPIRE WITH SEED, CROPS AND HORTICULTURAL EXPERTISE. QUEEN VICTORIA'S PATRONAGE SAW THE GARDENS FLOURISH; THE TEMPERATE HOUSE AND THE PALM HOUSE WERE BUILT AND THE NATIONAL ARBORETUM WAS FOUNDED.

Dauphine Foliage 73pt and Dauphine Regular 18pt

PAGODA

Dauphine Regular 159pt

FORMAL GARDENS

Dauphine Alternates 73pt

MONSIEUR GUILLAUME BEAUMONT TRAINED UNDER LE NÔTRE AT VERSAILLES AND LAID OUT THE GARDENS AT HAMPTON COURT.

Dauphine Regular 30pt

JARDIN BOTANIQUE
GATEHOUSE

Dauphine Regular 70pt and 99pt

LANDSCAPE DESIGNER AND ARTIST WILLIAM NESFIELD

Dauphine Foliage and Dauphine Alternates 23pt

QUEEN'S

Dauphine Regular 99pt

GLASSHOUSE

Dauphine Foliage 99pt

Dynasty Medium Italic 50pt

Nº5

Dynasty Thin 79pt

The beaches are deserted in winter and spring; deserted, that is, of human visitors. The local wildlife carries on its business uninterrupted, as it always has.

Dynasty Thin 8pt

The beaches are deserted in winter and spring; deserted, that is, of human visitors. The local wildlife carries on its business uninterrupted, as it always has.

Dynasty Thin Italic 8pt

Nº5

Dynasty Extra Light 79pt

The beaches are deserted in winter and spring; deserted, that is, of human visitors. The local wildlife carries on its business uninterrupted, as it always has.

Dynasty Extra Light 8pt

The beaches are deserted in winter and spring; deserted, that is, of human visitors. The local wildlife carries on its business uninterrupted, as it always has.

Dynasty Extra Light Italic 8pt

Nº5

Dynasty Light 79pt

The beaches are deserted in winter and spring; deserted, that is, of human visitors. The local wildlife carries on its business uninterrupted, as it always has.

Dynasty Light 8pt

The beaches are deserted in winter and spring; deserted, that is, of human visitors. The local wildlife carries on its business uninterrupted, as it always has.

Dynasty Light Italic 8pt

Nº5

Dynasty Medium 79pt

The beaches are deserted in winter and spring; deserted, that is, of human visitors. The local wildlife carries on its business uninterrupted, as it always has.

Dynasty Medium 8pt

The beaches are deserted in winter and spring; deserted, that is, of human visitors. The local wildlife carries on its business uninterrupted, as it always has.

Dynasty Medium Italic 8pt

Nº5

Dynasty Demi Bold 79pt

The beaches are deserted in winter and spring; deserted, that is, of human visitors. The local wildlife carries on its business uninterrupted, as it always has.

Dynasty Demi Bold 8pt

The beaches are deserted in winter and spring; deserted, that is, of human visitors. The local wildlife carries on its business uninterrupted, as it always has.

Dynasty Demi Bold Italic 8pt

Nº5

Dynasty Bold 79pt

The beaches are deserted in winter and spring; deserted, that is, of human visitors. The local wildlife carries on its business uninterrupted, as it always has.

Dynasty Bold 8pt

The beaches are deserted in winter and spring; deserted, that is, of human visitors. The local wildlife carries on its business uninterrupted, as it always has.

Dynasty Bold Italic 8pt

Nº5

Dynasty Heavy 79pt

The beaches are deserted in winter and spring; deserted, that is, of human visitors. The local wildlife carries on its business uninterrupted, as it always has.

Dynasty Heavy 8pt

The beaches are deserted in winter and spring; deserted, that is, of human visitors. The local wildlife carries on its business uninterrupted, as it always has.

Dynasty Heavy Italic 8pt

Tidal shores

Dynasty Medium 74pt

Camber Sands

Dynasty Thin 117pt and 140 pt

TURN LEFT FOR DUNGENESS POINT, a bleakly impressive jut of shale where the powerplant dwarfs the few other buildings.
Dynasty Thin and Thin Italic 13pt

TURN LEFT FOR DUNGENESS POINT, a bleakly impressive jut of shale where the powerplant dwarfs the few other buildings.
Dynasty Extra Light and Extra Light Italic

TURN LEFT FOR DUNGENESS POINT, a bleakly impressive jut of shale where the powerplant dwarfs the few other buildings.
Dynasty Light and Light Italic 13pt

TURN LEFT FOR DUNGENESS POINT, a bleakly impressive jut of shale where the powerplant dwarfs the few other buildings.
Dynasty Medium and Medium Italic 13pt

TURN LEFT FOR DUNGENESS POINT, a bleakly impressive jut of shale where the powerplant dwarfs the few other buildings.
Dynasty Demi Bold and Demi Bold Italic 13pt

TURN LEFT FOR DUNGENESS POINT, a bleakly impressive jut of shale where the powerplant dwarfs the few other buildings.
Dynasty Bold and Bold Italic 13pt

TURN LEFT FOR DUNGENESS POINT, a bleakly impressive jut of shale where the powerplant dwarfs the few other buildings.
Dynasty Heavy and Heavy Italic 13pt

SEASONS IN THE SUN

Dynasty Heavy 81pt

sub-micron

Drexler 88pt

advances in nanotechnology have put the manipulation of the very building blocks of life within reach, enabling the fabrication of an entire new generation of products that are cleaner, stronger, lighter, and more precise.

Drexler 20pt

nano

Drexler 191pt

Elegant Moderne

Egret Light 51pt

Traditional Ornament

Egret Light Flourish 40pt

Span traditional decorative typeface designs and geometric modernity in one family. One foot in the last century, the other in the century before.

Egret Light 9pt

Span traditional decorative typeface designs and geometric modernity in one family. One foot in the last century, the other in the century before.

Egret Light Flourish 9pt

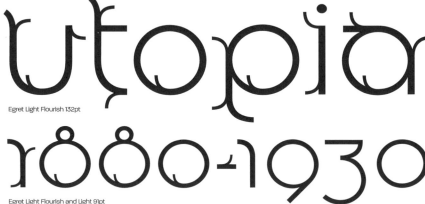

utopia

Egret Light Flourish 132pt

1880-1930

Egret Light Flourish and Light 91pt

Chic,
sleek and sophisticated

Electrasonic XX Fine 153pt and Fine 34pt

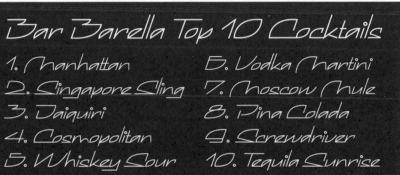

Bar Barella Top 10 Cocktails

1. *Manhattan*
2. *Singapore Sling*
3. *Daiquiri*
4. *Cosmopolitan*
5. *Whiskey Sour*
6. *Vodka Martini*
7. *Moscow Mule*
8. *Pina Colada*
9. *Screwdriver*
10. *Tequila Sunrise*

Electrasonic Fine 23pt and 16pt

Manhattan

Electrasonic Fine 62pt

Je T'aime · La Symphonie · Woman Ad Lib · Dancin'
Slow Dancing Disco · Boogie Underground · Get Down
Galaxy of Love · Hit the Dancefloor · Babe on Fire
I Love You · My Dream World · Cherry Lip Gloss
Friday Night "Something Special" · Don't Stop Lovin'

Electrasonic Fine, XX Fine and X Fine 13pt

Electrasonic Fine (with added drop shadow) 100pt

Galaxie Bold Italic 64pt

Droogo® AUDIO CIRCUITRY processes the surround channels derived by the multichannel decoder. *Virtual Speaker technology enables true-to-life 9.1 surround sound from both multichannel and stereo programs over as few as two speakers.*

Galaxie Bold, Light and Light Italic 11pt

Droogo® **AUDIO CIRCUITRY processes the surround channels derived by the multichannel decoder.** *Virtual Speaker technology enables true-to-life 9.1 surround sound from both multichannel and stereo programs over as few as two speakers.*

Galaxie Bold, Medium and Medium Italic 11pt

Full Frequency Response

Galaxie Bold and Light 26pt

Droogo® **AUDIO CIRCUITRY processes the surround channels derived by the multichannel decoder.** *Virtual Speaker technology enables true-to-life 9.1 surround sound from both multichannel and stereo programs over as few as two speakers.*

Galaxie Light, Bold and Bold Italic 11pt

Galaxie Bold 100pt and 22pt

Galaxie Light 21pt and Bold 35pt and 22pt

Its uniquely powerful signal processing convincingly portrays the sound of properly placed surround speakers, *making it ideal for use with computers, video players and widescreen sets.*

Galaxie Light and Light Italic 6pt

Its uniquely powerful signal processing convincingly portrays the sound of properly placed surround speakers, *making it ideal for use with computers, video players and widescreen sets.*

Galaxie Medium and Medium Italic 6pt

Its uniquely powerful signal processing convincingly portrays the sound of properly placed surround speakers, *making it ideal for use with computers, video players and widescreen sets.*

Galaxie Bold and Bold Italic 6pt

Empanada Gallega

Galicia Medium 33pt

They were fixed in her memory; the smooth beaches of *As Mariñas* and dangerous cliffs of *Costa de la Muerte*, the coast of death.

Galicia Medium, Light, Light Italic and Medium Italic 14pt

THESE SPANISH RIVERS CROSS THE WHOLE REGION from the mountainous inland to the coast. Thousands of pilgrims made their way to the cathedral of the newly founded town of Santiago de Compostela.

Galicia Light 6pt

THESE SPANISH RIVERS CROSS THE WHOLE REGION from the mountainous inland to the coast. Thousands of pilgrims made their way to the cathedral of the newly founded town of Santiago de Compostela.

Galicia Light Italic 6pt

THESE SPANISH RIVERS CROSS THE WHOLE REGION from the mountainous inland to the coast. Thousands of pilgrims made their way to the cathedral of the newly founded town of Santiago de Compostela.

Galicia Medium 6pt

THESE SPANISH RIVERS CROSS THE WHOLE REGION from the mountainous inland to the coast. Thousands of pilgrims made their way to the cathedral of the newly founded town of Santiago de Compostela.

Galicia Medium Italic 6pt

Santiago de Compostela

Galicia Medium 26pt

Rias Altas

Galicia Light 62pt

Thousands of pilgrims made their way to the cathedral of the newly founded town of *Santiago de Compostela.*

Galicia Light and Light Italic 17pt

Thousands of pilgrims made their way to the cathedral of the newly founded town of *Santiago de Compostela.*

Galicia Medium and Medium Italic 17pt

VITREOUS ENAMEL FLORAL ARRANGEMENTS

Galicia Medium 13pt

style leader

Gentry Bold 65pt

ELEGANT SOPHISTICATION INSTALLED AS STANDARD

Gentry Medium 32pt

EXECUTIVE RELIEF

Gentry Bold 41pt

The Concept, the culmination of four years of research and development and the ultimate expression of luxury, was unveiled today at the Monte Carlo Motor Show. The Concept is a powerful but understated executive car with unique

Gentry Medium 13pt

The Concept, the culmination of four years of research and development and the ultimate expression of luxury, was unveiled today at the Monte Carlo Motor Show. The Concept is a powerful but understated executive car

Gentry Bold 13pt

Moustache Twirling and Tea Drinking

Gentry Medium 45pt

FUTURE PROOF

Gentry Bold 97pt

docking station

Gentry Bold 50pt

Two snow-white tigers strut through the dry ice spilling out over the dancefloor. Behind, dressed in 5-inch heels and a toreador hat, Gloria Jo tugs on their diamond encrusted leads like a bareback horserider.

Glitterati Light 34pt

The music rises to a crescendo; the chic set have just arrived on the dancefloor. Hot, sexy and hedonistic, these gorgeous young sophisticates will groove till 6am.

Glitterati Alternates 19pt

AAEEFFHHQQXXSS
WW&&eeggsww

Glitterati Light and Alternates mixed 73pt

SSOOTTOOoceesstteb

Glitterati Alternates 52pt. Glitterati Alternates features numerous kerned ligatures

THE MUSIC RISES TO A CRESCENDO; THE CHIC SET HAVE JUST ARRIVED ON THE DANCEFLOOR. HOT, SEXY AND HEDONISTIC, THESE GORGEOUS YOUNG SOPHISTICATES WILL GROOVE TILL 6AM.

Glitterati Light 17pt

THE MUSIC RISES TO A CRESCENDO; THE CHIC SET HAVE JUST ARRIVED ON THE DANCEFLOOR. HOT, SEXY AND HEDONISTIC, THESE GORGEOUS YOUNG SOPHISTICATES WILL GROOVE TILL 6AM.

Glitterati Alternates 17pt

PAPARAZZI

Glitterati Light and Alternates 108pt

FAT CHANCE

Gusto Highlight 201pt and Gusto Regular 90pt

A CORNUCOPIA OF CHOCOLATE DELIGHTS

SEDUCE YOUR SENSES WITH AN ARRAY OF ALLURING AROMAS, INCOMPARABLE FLAVOURS AND TEMPTING TEXTURES.

Gusto Regular 32pt and 17pt

CHOCOLATE FUDGE

Gusto Highlight 62pt and Gusto Solid 112pt

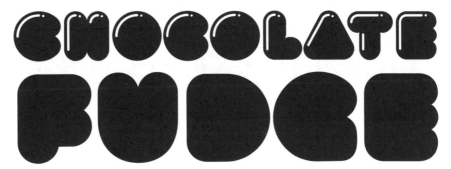

A CORNUCOPIA OF CHOCOLATE DELIGHTS

SEDUCE YOUR SENSES WITH AN ARRAY OF ALLURING AROMAS, INCOMPARABLE FLAVOURS AND TEMPTING TEXTURES.

Gusto Highlight 32pt and Gusto Solid 17pt

CUSTOM METALLIC PAINT JOB

Interceptor Nitro 21pt

FUEL INJECTION

Interceptor Regular 133pt and 63pt

ROLLING IN A 1985 SKODA HI-JET ● TRICKED-OUT HUMMERS AND FERRARIS ● OVERHEAD CAMSHAFT

Interceptor Regular and Italic 12pt

17-INCH CHROME RIMS, MINI-FRIDGE, OPTICS IN THE REAR, GUITAR AMP, SIX-DVD CHANGER

Interceptor Italic 19pt

TIME FOR A JOY RIDE.

Interceptor Nitro Italic 29pt

PLASMA SCREEN CODED DIGITAL

Monitor Regular 35pt

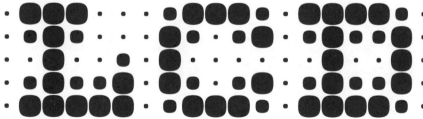

Monitor Regular 149pt

WIDESCREEN SIGNAL FORMAT. IHOME CENTRAL WIRELESS HUB TECHNOLOGY MP3 DEDICATED HARD DRIVE CAPACITY AUTONOMOUS REMOTE SUBSYSTEM

Monitor Regular 15pt

TRANSMISSION

Monitor Regular 36pt

BERKELEY SQUARE
LEADING TO
NEW COLLEGE HILL PRINCESS PLACE

Ministry Medium 30pt and Extra Bold 15pt

C-ZONE ENTRY Meter parking and resident permit holders only. Monday to Friday: 9 am to 6 pm. No waiting. Loading restricted to designated bays. Motor vehicles under I.5 tons, buses and Hackney Carriages excepted.

Ministry Bold 7pt

C-ZONE ENTRY Meter parking and resident permit holders only. Monday to Friday: 9 am to 6 pm. No waiting. Loading restricted to designated bays. Motor vehicles under I.5 tons, buses and Hackney Carriages excepted.

Ministry Bold Italic 7pt

C-ZONE ENTRY Meter parking and resident permit holders only. Monday to Friday: 9 am to 6 pm. No waiting. Loading restricted to designated bays. Motor vehicles under I.5 tons, buses and Hackney Carriages excepted.

Ministry Extra Bold 7pt

C-ZONE ENTRY Meter parking and resident permit holders only. Monday to Friday: 9 am to 6 pm. No waiting. Loading restricted to designated bays. Motor vehicles under I.5 tons, buses and Hackney Carriages excepted.

Ministry Extra Bold Italic 7pt

C-ZONE ENTRY Meter parking and resident permit holders only. Monday to Friday: 9 am to 6 pm. No waiting. Loading restricted to designated bays. Motor vehicles under I.5 tons, buses and Hackney Carriages excepted.

Ministry Heavy 7pt

C-ZONE ENTRY Meter parking and resident permit holders only. Monday to Friday: 9 am to 6 pm. No waiting. Loading restricted to designated bays. Motor vehicles under I.5 tons, buses and Hackney Carriages excepted.

Ministry Heavy Italic 7pt

NO THROUGH ROAD
Speed limit on bridge 5 m.p.h for vehicles over 5 tons gross weight. **KEEP LEFT**

Ministry Extra Bold and Ministry Light 19pt

TO CAR PARK

Ministry Medium 25pt

LOW BRIDGE
14'-0"
HEADROOM

Ministry Medium 21pt and 32pt

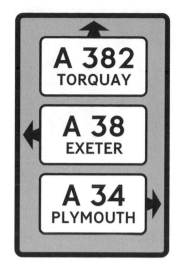

Ministry Bold 96pt

Ministry Medium 21pt and 13pt

WINCHESTER ¾
WORTHING ½
CHICHESTER ¼

Ministry Medium 45pt

C-ZONE ENTRY Meter parking and resident permit holders only Monday to Friday: 9 am to 6 pm. No waiting Loading restricted to designated bays. Motor vehicles under 15 tons, buses and Hackney Carriages excepted.

Ministry Thin 7pt

C-ZONE ENTRY Meter parking and resident permit holders only. Monday to Friday: 9 am to 6 pm. No waiting. Loading restricted to designated bays. Motor vehicles under 1.5 tons, buses and Hackney Carriages excepted.

Ministry Extra Light 7pt

C-ZONE ENTRY Meter parking and resident permit holders only. Monday to Friday: 9 am to 6 pm. No waiting. Loading restricted to designated bays. Motor vehicles under 1.5 tons, buses and Hackney Carriages excepted.

Ministry Light 7pt

C-ZONE ENTRY Meter parking and resident permit holders only. Monday to Friday: 9 am to 6 pm. No waiting. Loading restricted to designated bays. Motor vehicles under 1.5 tons, buses and Hackney Carriages excepted.

Ministry Medium 7pt

C-ZONE ENTRY Meter parking and resident permit holders only Monday to Friday: 9 am to 6 pm. No waiting. Loading restricted to designated bays. Motor vehicles under 15 tons, buses and Hackney Carriages excepted

Ministry Thin Italic 7pt

C-ZONE ENTRY Meter parking and resident permit holders only. Monday to Friday: 9 am to 6 pm. No waiting. Loading restricted to designated bays. Motor vehicles under 1.5 tons, buses and Hackney Carriages excepted.

Ministry Extra Light Italic 7pt

C-ZONE ENTRY Meter parking and resident permit holders only. Monday to Friday: 9 am to 6 pm. No waiting. Loading restricted to designated bays. Motor vehicles under 1.5 tons, buses and Hackney Carriages excepted.

Ministry Light Italic 7pt

C-ZONE ENTRY Meter parking and resident permit holders only. Monday to Friday: 9 am to 6 pm. No waiting. Loading restricted to designated bays. Motor vehicles under 1.5 tons, buses and Hackney Carriages excepted.

Ministry Medium Italic 7pt

Regesto

Miserichordia Regular 163pt

Contesto ricerca ✲ 1432 settembre 5 Prestito di legname alla Miserichordia

Miserichordia Regular 15pt

The fall of the Venetian Republic in 1797

Miserichordia Regular and alternates '1797' 30pt

Couchette de luxe, PARIS [Gare du Nord] to VENICE

Miserichordia Regular and alternates 'Venice' 24pt

Virtuosi di Roma {La Fenice Theatre} Frezzerie

Miserichordia Regular 25pt

Riva di Biasio ✻ Serenissima

Miserichordia alternatives 42pt

First a latté in the elegant Gran Caffé Lavena, preferred café of Wagner, then Dinner Dansant in costume in the elegant Ballroom of the Hotel Bauer, next to San Marco Square, where a Master of Dance and a baroque ensemble provides music for minuets, waltzes and quadrilles.

Miserichordia Regular 17pt

Gothic complex

Miserichordia alternatives 79pt

Princess honour guard of mystical realms

Moonstone Starlight 27pt

Violet Midnight

Moonstone Starlight 72pt

Out of the abyss she came, resplendent in sunfire and moondust and trailing her entourage of strange and unseemly beasts. Long ago, they had pledged their service to her - in nameless adventures in pinwheel galaxies without number, galaxies whose light will remain hidden from human eyes for millennia hence.

Moonstone Regular 21pt

Wicca Magic Coven #13

Moonstone Starlight 45pt

SPARKLE

Moonstone Regular 124pt

CHARM BRACELET

Moonstone Starlight 59pt

EATON GARDENS

Mulgrave 36pt

METALHEAD CRITTER

Mulgrave 35pt

R & T RAILWAY COMPANY.

PERSONS USING THIS CROSSING ARE
STRICTLY FORBIDDEN
TO GO NEAR THE RAILS PROVIDED FOR SUPPLYING
ELECTRIC CURRENT.
ANYONE TRESPASSING IN THIS MANNER DOES
SO ENTIRELY AT THEIR OWN RISK.
BY ORDER

258-A

Mulgrave 12, 18 and 24pt

CAST IRON

Mulgrave 70pt

AYNDAY WOAD W.5

Mulgrave 42 and 16pt

THOMAS THWAITE C⁰. LTD

IMPROVED OPERATION

MANUFACTURED BY RAMSEY & SON.
INVERNESS – CARDIFF – LONDON

Mulgrave 19 and 63pt

X-3000 HARDWARE and WETWARE IMPLANT UPGRADES

Outlander Nova Black and Outlander Nova Light 23pt

OUTLANDER NOVA PROVIDES NEW UPPER-CASE CHARACTERS (A, E, T, Y) IN ADDITION TO THE UNICASE VERSIONS PREVIOUSLY AVAILABLE (a, e, t, y). THE UNICASE CHARACTERS NOW OCCUPY THE LOWER-CASE CHARACTER KEYSTROKES. K AND X ARE PROVIDED WITH ALTERNATE VERSIONS: K, X. THE LETTER "U" HAS BEEN REDESIGNED TO PROVIDE GREATER VISUAL DIFFERENTIATION FROM THE "V".

Outlander Nova Black Italic, Outlander Nova Black and Outlander Nova Medium Italic 10pt

e.v.a.

Outlander Nova Medium 105pt

ARMAMENT MANUFACTURE & YOUTH MARKETING

Outlander Nova Medium Italic 27pt

altair

Outlander Nova Black 76pt

FULL BODY BATTLEDRESS

Outlander Nova Black Italic 19pt

1. STARSYSTEM REVENUE ESTIMATION
2. INDIGENOUS INHABITANT REMOVAL
3. ECOSYSTEM EXTERMINATION
4. MINERAL EXTRACTION AND DISPOSAL

Outlander Nova Black and Outlander Nova Light 13pt

SUBSPACE RELAY TECHSUPPORT

Outlander Nova Black 29pt

MODEL X-1

Outlander Nova Black 29pt

THE DATABASE CONTAINS INFORMATION ON THE VARIOUS CARGO HOLDS AVAILABLE ON EACH OUTBOUND AIRPLANE.

Payload Spraycan 14pt

FREIGHT

Payload Spraycan 92pt

● FLIGHT ID ● CARGO HOLD ● CONTENTS ● CLASSIFICATION

1354 A BOOTS UNCLASSIFIED
1354 B GUNS UNCLASSIFIED
1354 C BIOWEAPON TOP SECRET

Payload Regular 9pt and 16pt

№1354

Payload Regular 90pt

THIS NUMBER MAY BE CROSS-REFERENCED WITH OTHER TABLES TO DETERMINE THE ORIGIN, DESTINATION, FLIGHT TIME AND OTHER RELATED DATA.

Payload Regular 25pt

Payload Outline 50pt

ORGANIC TEA

Payload Wide Outline 31pt

X-1 EXPERIMENTAL JET

Payload Wide 17pt

BLACK OPS EXTRACTION
MAXIMUM DENIABILITY
HUEY EVAC IMMINENT

Payload Narrow 20pt

BLACK OPS EXTRACTION
MAXIMUM DENIABILITY
HUEY EVAC IMMINENT

Payload Narrow Outline 20pt

TARGET
CONTAINER

23
HEAVY LOAD

Payload Narrow 93pt and Payload Wide 10pt and 50pt

FACT & FICTION

Payload Narrow, Payload Wide and Payload Narrow Outline 60pt

RESUPPLY COMMAND
DROP ZONE

Payload Wide Outline 19pt and Payload Wide 36pt

FAIR
TRADE
PRODUCE
SUPPLIES
MARKED
HESSIAN
BAGS &
FIRST AID

Payload Wide and Payload Wide Outline 7pt

FAIR
TRADE
PRODUCE
SUPPLIES
MARKED
HESSIAN
BAGS &
FIRST AID

Payload Wide Outline and Payload Wide 7pt

MERLOT

Pitshanger Initial Capitals 142pt

HOROLOGER BIJOUTERIE

Scents of plums, black cherry, toffee, chocolate, violets, orange and tea.

Pitshanger Regular 45pt and Pitshanger Regular with Initial Capitals 'S' 15pt

Egyptian caryatids of Coade Stone, painted bronze, supporting a shallow domed ceiling painted with a turquoise and peach sky.

Pitshanger Regular with Initial Capitals 'E' 17pt

Rue VICTOR HUGO

Pitshanger Regular and Initial Capitals 56pt

CHÂTEAU

Pitshanger Initial Capitals 120pt

Soane's elegant Pitshanger Manor {1768} ✦ GEORGE DANCE WING
Classical exterior ❖ Ionic pillars ❖ Female figures on entablatures

Pitshanger Initial Capitals and Regular 16pt

EAGLES in wreaths; roundels, lions and cherubs

Pitshanger Initial Capitals and Regular 22pt

valve?

Radiogram Tall 297pt

wax paper contacts, walnut cabinet, crystal receiver

Radiogram Solid 28pt

City Radio Wireless

Radiogram Solid Tall 79pt

Heavy mains hum and audible audio distortion

Radiogram Regular 34pt

One to three short wavebands with fine bandspread tuning
MEDIUM AND LONG WAVE | SWITCHED BASS AND TREBLE CONTROLS

Radiogram Solid Regular 26pt

Aysgarth luminous dials

Radiogram Solid Regular and Tall (ascenders only) 64pt

RHEOSTAT

Radiogram Regular 179pt

Template

Ritafurey Extra Light 88pt

AN IDEALIZED PROTOTYPE for what American suburbs might have become.

Ritafurey Thin Italic and Ritafurey Thin 20pt

AN IDEALIZED PROTOTYPE for what American suburbs might have become.

Ritafurey Extra Light Italic and Extra Light 20pt

AN IDEALIZED PROTOTYPE for what American suburbs might have become.

Ritafurey Light Italic and Ritafurey Light 20pt

AN IDEALIZED PROTOTYPE for what American suburbs might have become.

Ritafurey Medium Italic and Ritafurey Medium 20pt

AN IDEALIZED PROTOTYPE **for what American suburbs might have become.**

Ritafurey Demi Bold Italic and Ritafurey Demi Bold 20pt

AN IDEALIZED PROTOTYPE **for what American suburbs might have become.**

Ritafurey Bold Italic and Ritafurey Bold 20pt

Blueprints

PERSPECTIVES DEMONSTRATE BUILDINGS AND ROADWAYS AS AN INTEGRATED TOTALITY.

Ritafurey Bold 75pt and Bold Italic 20pt

Plan

Ritafurey Medium 188pt

THE RELATIONSHIP between architecture and the human experience is one that encompasses memory, play, innovation, comfort, security and curiosity.

Ritafurey Thin 9pt

THE RELATIONSHIP between architecture and the human experience is one that encompasses memory, play, innovation, comfort, security and curiosity.

Ritafurey Extra Light 9pt

THE RELATIONSHIP between architecture and the human experience is one that encompasses memory, play, innovation, comfort, security and curiosity.

Ritafurey Light 9pt

THE RELATIONSHIP between architecture and the human experience is one that encompasses memory, play, innovation, comfort, security and curiosity.

Ritafurey Medium 9pt

THE RELATIONSHIP between architecture and the human experience is one that encompasses memory, play, innovation, comfort, security and curiosity.

Ritafurey Demi Bold 9pt

THE RELATIONSHIP between architecture and the human experience is one that encompasses memory, play, innovation, comfort, security and curiosity.

Ritafurey Bold 9pt

THE RELATIONSHIP between architecture and the human experience is one that encompasses memory, play, innovation, comfort, security and curiosity.

Ritafurey Thin Italic 9pt

THE RELATIONSHIP between architecture and the human experience is one that encompasses memory, play, innovation, comfort, security and curiosity.

Ritafurey Extra Light Italic 9pt

THE RELATIONSHIP between architecture and the human experience is one that encompasses memory, play, innovation, comfort, security and curiosity.

Ritafurey Light Italic 9pt

THE RELATIONSHIP between architecture and the human experience is one that encompasses memory, play, innovation, comfort, security and curiosity.

Ritafurey Medium Italic 9pt

THE RELATIONSHIP between architecture and the human experience is one that encompasses memory, play, innovation, comfort, security and curiosity.

Ritafurey Demi Bold Italic 9pt

THE RELATIONSHIP between architecture and the human experience is one that encompasses memory, play, innovation, comfort, security and curiosity.

Ritafurey Bold Italic 9pt

NET SLIDE

Ritafurey Thin 56pt

ELEVATION

Ritafurey Extra Light 56pt

FLOOR PLAN

Ritafurey Light 56pt

EMERGENCY

Ritafurey Medium 56pt

BREAKOUT

Ritafurey Demi Bold 56pt

STRUCTURAL

Ritafurey Bold 56pt

RIOT!

Roadkill 300pt

A TYPEFACE DERIVED FROM HONG KONG PAINTED ROAD MARKINGS

Roadkill 24pt

KENNEDY OVERPASS
WALLACE BUILDING

Roadkill 83pt

THE ROAD COMPANY MAY BY THE ERECTION OR PLACING OF AN
APPROPRIATE SIGN CANCEL, ALTER OR TEMPORARILY SUSPEND
THE OPERATION OF ANY TRAFFIC SIGN OR ROAD MARKING
ERECTED OR PLACED UNDER SUBREGULATION (16), (2) OR (5).
OBSERVATION OF ANY TEMPORARY SIGN IS MANDATORY.

Roadkill 20pt

BUS
STOP

Roadkill 47pt

KOWLOON HK AGENDA

Roadkill 67pt

This amount **$26.5m** represents the balance of the total contract value executed on behalf of the Department. Contract costs have been paid to the contractor, and the balance amounting to the said figure has in principle been approved to be remitted by Telegraphic Transfer (T.T). Please therefore fill in an application for the transfer of rights and privileges of the aforesaid contractor to you.

Rogue Serif Light 22pt and Rogue Serif Medium 79pt

Telegraphic Transfer

Rogue Serif Light 70pt

ONCE THE NON-DICLOSURE AGREEMENTS are in place the new globalisation policy document can be presented.

Rogue Serif Light 9pt

ONCE THE NON-DICLOSURE AGREEMENTS are in place the new globalisation policy document can be presented.

Rogue Serif Medium 9pt

ONCE THE NON-DICLOSURE AGREEMENTS are in place the new globalisation policy document can be presented.

Rogue Serif Bold 9pt

ONCE THE NON-DICLOSURE AGREEMENTS are in place the new globalisation policy document can be presented.

Rogue Serif Light Italic 9pt

ONCE THE NON-DICLOSURE AGREEMENTS are in place the new globalisation policy document can be presented.

Rogue Serif Medium Italic 9pt

ONCE THE NON-DICLOSURE AGREEMENTS are in place the new globalisation policy document can be presented.

Rogue Serif Bold Italic 9pt

Rights and Privileges

Rogue Serif Bold 39pt

Transportation infrastructure; urban regeneration initiatives; suburban malls, cafés and new build entertainment complexes.
Rogue Sans Light 9pt

Transportation infrastructure; urban regeneration initiatives; suburban malls, cafés and new build entertainment complexes.
Rogue Sans Medium 9pt

Transportation infrastructure; urban regeneration initiatives; suburban malls, cafés and new build entertainment complexes.
Rogue Sans Bold 9pt

Transportation infrastructure; urban regeneration initiatives; suburban malls, cafés and new build entertainment complexes.
Rogue Sans Light Italic 9pt

Transportation infrastructure; urban regeneration initiatives; suburban malls, cafés and new build entertainment complexes.
Rogue Sans Medium Italic 9pt

Transportation infrastructure; urban regeneration initiatives; suburban malls, cafés and new build entertainment complexes.
Rogue Sans Bold Italic 9pt

Balance
Rogue Sans Bold 115pt

CAUTION: Do not point the HYPERBALLISTIC DISRUPTOR™ at plants, pets, family members or government officials.
Rogue Sans Light 15pt

CAUTION: Do not point the HYPERBALLISTIC DISRUPTOR™ at plants, pets, family members or government officials.
Rogue Sans Light Italic 15pt

CAUTION: Do not point the HYPERBALLISTIC DISRUPTOR™ at plants, pets, family members or government officials.
Rogue Sans Medium 15pt

CAUTION: Do not point the HYPERBALLISTIC DISRUPTOR™ at plants, pets, family members or government officials.
Rogue Sans Medium Italic 15pt

CAUTION: Do not point the HYPERBALLISTIC DISRUPTOR™ at plants, pets, family members or government officials.
Rogue Sans Bold 15pt

CAUTION: Do not point the HYPERBALLISTIC DISRUPTOR™ at plants, pets, family members or government officials.
Rogue Sans Bold Italic 15pt

Rogue Sans Light Italic 93pt

Corporate Banking

Rogue Sans Extended Medium 73pt and 87pt

IPS manages relationships with banks, large corporations, financial institutions and government bodies. We operate in *Europe, Australia, New Zealand, New York, Bangkok, Hong Kong, Singapore* and *Tokyo*. **IPS Corporate Banking Services** has dedicated staff to provide accessible management for customers.

Rogue Sans Extended Bold, Light and Light Italic 18pt

BANGKOK, SYDNEY, LONDON AND NEW YORK

Rogue Sans Extended Medium 38pt and 68pt

IPS CORPORATE BANKING SERVICES provides debt financing, high risk management, investor services and products.

Rogue Sans Extended Light 8pt

IPS CORPORATE BANKING SERVICES provides debt financing, high risk management, investor services and products.

Rogue Sans Extended Medium 8pt

IPS CORPORATE BANKING SERVICES provides debt financing, high risk management, investor services and products.

Rogue Sans Extended Bold 8pt

IPS CORPORATE BANKING SERVICES provides debt financing, high risk management, investor services and products.

Rogue Sans Extended Light Italic 8pt

IPS CORPORATE BANKING SERVICES provides debt financing, high risk management, investor services and products.

Rogue Sans Extended Medium Italic 8pt

IPS CORPORATE BANKING SERVICES provides debt financing, high risk management, investor services and products.

Rogue Sans Extended Bold Italic 8pt

Accessible Management

Rogue Sans Extended Medium 28pt

OUR UNIQUE VIRAL MARKETING CAMPAIGNS are proven to place your product or service in an unbeatable global position.

Rogue Sans Condensed Light 10pt

OUR UNIQUE VIRAL MARKETING CAMPAIGNS are proven to place your product or service in an unbeatable global position.

Rogue Sans Condensed Medium 10pt

OUR UNIQUE VIRAL MARKETING CAMPAIGNS are proven to place your product or service in an unbeatable global position.

Rogue Sans Condensed Bold 10pt

OUR UNIQUE VIRAL MARKETING CAMPAIGNS are proven to place your product or service in an unbeatable global position.

Rogue Sans Condensed Light Italic 10pt

OUR UNIQUE VIRAL MARKETING CAMPAIGNS are proven to place your product or service in an unbeatable global position.

Rogue Sans Condensed Medium Italic 10pt

OUR UNIQUE VIRAL MARKETING CAMPAIGNS are proven to place your product or service in an unbeatable global position.

Rogue Sans Condensed Bold Italic 10pt

Aquisitions & Mergers

Rogue Sans Condensed Bold and Light 47pt

IPS CORPORATE BANKING SERVICES provides debt financing, high risk management, investor services and products.

Rogue Sans Condensed Light 17pt

IPS CORPORATE BANKING SERVICES provides debt financing, high risk management, investor services and products.

Rogue Sans Condensed Light Italic 17pt

IPS CORPORATE BANKING SERVICES provides debt financing, high risk management, investor services and products.

Rogue Sans Condensed Medium 17pt

IPS CORPORATE BANKING SERVICES provides debt financing, high risk management, investor services and products.

Rogue Sans Condensed Medium Italic 17pt

IPS CORPORATE BANKING SERVICES provides debt financing, high risk management, investor services and products.

Rogue Sans Condensed Bold 17pt

IPS CORPORATE BANKING SERVICES provides debt financing, high risk management, investor services and products.

Rogue Sans Condensed Bold Italic 17pt

TRIPLE STAR

Finance

Rogue Sans Condensed Light 164pt and Rogue Sans Condensed Bold 17pt

Science vs
Séance

September Heavy and Heavy Italic 79pt and 114pt

THE EPITOME OF DECADENCE AND ELEGANCE, a séance is the perfect 1800s *French Quarter* society entertainment. Book one for a relaxed comfortable evening, before or after dinner.

September Medium and Medium Italic 8pt

THE EPITOME OF DECADENCE AND ELEGANCE, a séance is the perfect 1800s *French Quarter* society entertainment. Book one for a relaxed comfortable evening, before or after dinner.

September Bold and Bold Italic 8pt

THE EPITOME OF DECADENCE AND ELEGANCE, a séance is the perfect 1800s *French Quarter* society entertainment. Book one for a relaxed comfortable evening, before or after dinner.

September Heavy and Heavy Italic 8pt

THE EPITOME OF DECADENCE AND ELEGANCE, a séance is the perfect 1800s French Quarter society entertainment. Book one for a relaxed comfortable evening, before or after dinner.

September Medium Italic and Medium 8pt

THE EPITOME OF DECADENCE AND ELEGANCE, a séance is the perfect 1800s French Quarter society entertainment. Book one for a relaxed comfortable evening, before or after dinner.

September Bold Italic and Bold 8pt

THE EPITOME OF DECADENCE AND ELEGANCE, a séance is the perfect 1800s French Quarter society entertainment. Book one for a relaxed comfortable evening, before or after dinner.

September Heavy Italic and Heavy 8pt

Venture

September Heavy Italic 105pt

RESPONSE
CONTROL
HANDLING

September Medium. Bold and Heavy 78pt

United front

September Medium and Medium Italic 76pt

MORECAMBE

Sparrowhawk 60pt

A GLITTERING ARRAY OF STAR~STUDDED TALENT! BOOK YOUR SEAT AT THE WEST PIER GALA VARIETY PERFORMANCE NOW!

Sparrowhawk 25pt

BLUSTER

Sparrowhawk 93pt

YORK

Sparrowhawk 140pt

GREAT YARMOUTH LOCOMOTIVE MUSEUM • ROLLING STOCK • CRAZY GOLF
PIRATE SHIP • FAMILY FUN RESTAURANT • CAROUSEL • HALL OF MIRRORS

Sparrowhawk 11pt

BANK HOLIDAY

Sparrowhawk 53pt

ST. SWITHINS

Sparrowhawk 63pt

£3.50

Sparrowhawk 170pt

smoked glass ⌐ble,
drop-pendant lights,
vinyl upholstery &
marshmallow couch:
tangerine daydream!

Straker 39pt

uforia

Straker with added drop shadow 135pt

Apollo-Soyuz

Straker 66pt

Cosmonauts of the Red Spaceguard, 1999-2140

Straker 18pt

injection moulding

Straker 45pt

TYRANT OF THE OUTER RIMWORLDS

Straker 27pt

Beige

Straker Regular 160pt

MINDSWAP TRANSFER TERMINUS

Telstar 46pt

analogue

Telstar 175pt

Aldrin Lunar Base, Sea of Tranquillity

Telstar 40pt

Dateline September 15th, 1969: Nixon approves manned Mars mission. ETA: November 12th, 1981

Telstar 16pt

PRESSURISED AIRLOCK

Telstar 70pt

Through a filter sensitive to wavelengths of ultraviolet light centered at 938 nanometers, Titan appears as a softly glowing sphere encircled in a purple stratospheric haze of methane and nitrogen molecules. These products react to form complex organic molecules containing carbon, hydrogen and nitrogen.

Telstar 14pt

Space Tug

Telstar 168pt

Spectral Camera

Telstar 14pt

Image scale: 6.7 kilometers (2.9 miles) per pixel

Telstar 14pt

Journal La presse

Valise Montréal 92pt

Paul Chomedey de Maisonneuve's defense of the young French settlement against the Iroquois

Valise Montréal 17pt

BREATHLESS

Valise Montréal 96pt

BLOOD BROTHERS foxfurs

Valise Montréal 67pt

The opulent and classic elements of the original 1880 cherry wood structure have been stylishly intermixed with modern chocolate and cheese cocktail glamour. The boudoir featured glamour pin-up and Vanity Fair fashion images.

Valise Montréal 21pt

Girlfriend

Valise Montréal 180pt

Notre-Dame Basilica • Minimalist touches • Continental breakfast

Valise Montréal 24pt

Place d'Armes

Valise Montréal 120pt

interface

Xenotype Regular 174pt

THE FREE ENERGY PROFILES AT THE WATER LIQUID-VAPOR INTERFACE AT 910 K ARE CALCULATED USING MOLECULAR DYNAMICS COMPUTER SIMULATIONS.

Xenotype Regular 27pt

The mysterious Cosmological Constant, the term Einstein introduced and later repudiated, has now been resurrected. This constant represents a form of energy that permeates empty space and drives the expansion of the universe.

Xenotype Regular 27pt

The formation of the solution structure around the micromolecule and the time evolution of the probability distribution is located at the interface described by the diffusion equation on the free energy surface.

Xenotype Regular 18pt

Biology

Xenotype Shaded 233pt

Pixellate

Yellow Perforated 71pt

STAMP DUTY

Yellow Perforated Solid 49pt

Penny black uncut complete sheet

Yellow Perforated Solid and Yellow Perforated 18pt

Postal address

Yellow Perforated 41pt

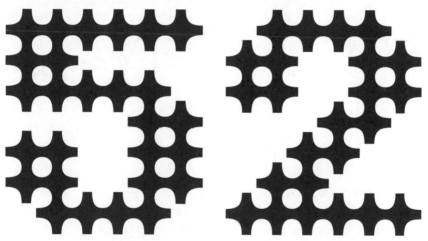

Yellow Perforated Solid 250pt

Automatic gauge defined

Yellow Perforated Solid 25pt

Perforated eardrum

Yellow Perforated 31pt

Genuine fast-track ticketing service
and customer defined seat allocation
as standard. Automatic secure gate
checking and luggage forwarding
software preinstalled.

Yellow Perforated 17pt

DF Yolanda → Full family listing page 86

Palace Grounds

Yolanda Princess 66pt

Brocade drapes separated the boudour from the salon

Yolanda Duchess 18pt

Queen B

Yolanda Duchess 117pt

Jagielon Liechtenstein Limburg Lorraine Mecklenburg Schwarzburg & Toulouse

Yolanda Duchess 13pt

Crystal Tiara

Yolanda Duchess 'C' and Yolanda Countess 78pt

The ballroom, of course, was quite her favourite room; as miniature fireworks, the chandeliers reflected the sparkles thrown from the dizzyingly colourful attire of the fine young things dancing below. She recognised noble blood from a dozen dynasties, all of whom were sharing the evening as old friends.

Yolanda Princess Drop 'T' 45pt and Yolanda Countess 12pt

CHAISE-LONGUE

Yolanda Countess 58pt

SHE HELD THE MASK LIGHTLY; A RAISED EYEBROW WAS VISIBLE ABOVE. "I INSIST YOU ACCOMPANY ME TO THE GAMES ROOM" SHE STATED. SHE WAS OBVIOUSLY A WOMAN UNFAMILIAR WITH BEING DENIED.

Yolanda Countess 13pt

Merovingian

Yolanda Princess 82pt

CITY SCANDAL BANK CHAOS

Zond Diktat 45pt

Zond Diktat 39pt

Zond Diktat 55pt and Zond Diktat Heavy 67pt

FREEDOM NOW!

Zond Diktat 73pt

LATEST

Zond Diktat 90pt

DIVA OSCAR SENSATION FULL PICTURE REPORT

Zond Diktat 19pt

PROTEST

Zond Diktat Heavy 77pt

TALES FROM THE RAGING BULL: TWENTY YEARS OF 'KULCHA' ON A TOWER HAMLETS SINK ESTATE

Zond Diktat Heavy 15pt

DF Absinthe

Regular

THE QUICK BROWN FOX JUMPS OVER THE LAZY DOG.
THE QUICK BROWN FOX JUMPS OVER THE LAZY DOG.

THE QUICK BROWN FOX JUMPS OVER THE LAZY DOG.
THE QUICK BROWN FOX JUMPS OVER THE LAZY DOG.

THE QUICK BROWN FOX JUMPS OVER THE LAZY DOG.
THE QUICK BROWN FOX JUMPS OVER THE LAZY DOG.

ABCDEFGHIJKLMNOPQRSTUVWXYZ ABCDEFGHIJKLMNO
PQRSTUVWXYZ 1234567890 ,.;:?!%£$¢&NO°(())·@©

DF Box Office

Regular

★ ★★ ★★★ ★★★★ ★★★★★ ★★★★★★

DF Catseye

Medium
Medium Italic
Bold
Bold Italic

Ea1

The quick brown fox jumps over the lazy dog.
THE QUICK BROWN FOX JUMPS OVER THE LAZY DOG.

The quick brown fox jumps over the lazy dog.
THE QUICK BROWN FOX JUMPS OVER THE LAZY DOG.

The quick brown fox jumps over the lazy dog.
THE QUICK BROWN FOX JUMPS OVER THE LAZY D

ABCDEFGHIJKLMNOPQRSTUVWXYZ
abcdefghijklmnopqrstuvwxyz
1234567890 ,.;:?!%£$¢&#[[]]@©

ABCDEFGHIJKLMNOPQRSTUVWXYZ
abcdefghijklmnopqrstuvwxyz
1234567890 ,.;:?!%£$¢&#[[]]@©

ABCDEFGHIJKLMNOPQRSTUVWXYZ
abcdefghijklmnopqrstuvwxyz
1234567890 ,.;:?!%£$¢&#[[]]@©

ABCDEFGHIJKLMNOPQRSTUVWXYZ
abcdefghijklmnopqrstuvwxyz
1234567890 ,.;:?!%£$¢&#-[[]]@©

DF Catseye Narrow

Narrow
Narrow Italic

The quick brown fox jumps over the lazy dog.
THE QUICK BROWN FOX JUMPS OVER THE LAZY DOG.
The quick brown fox jumps over the lazy dog.
THE QUICK BROWN FOX JUMPS OVER THE LAZY DOG.
The quick brown fox jumps over the lazy dog.
THE QUICK BROWN FOX JUMPS OVER THE LAZY DOG.

ABCDEFGHIJKLMNOPQRSTUVWXYZ
abcdefghijklmnopqrstuvwxyz
1234567890 ,.;:?!%£$¢&#[[]]@©

ABCDEFGHIJKLMNOPQRSTUVWXYZ
abcdefghijklmnopqrstuvwxyz
1234567890 ,.;:?!%£$¢&#[[]]@©

Dipple *Chronicles*

Catseye Narrow Italic 57 pt

DF Chantal

Light
Light Italic
Medium
Medium Italic
Bold
Bold Italic

THE QUICK BROWN FOX JUMPS OVER THE LAZY DOG.
THE QUICK BROWN FOX JUMPS OVER THE LAZY DOG.

THE QUICK BROWN FOX JUMPS OVER THE LAZY DOG.
THE QUICK BROWN FOX JUMPS OVER THE LAZY DOG.

THE QUICK BROWN FOX JUMPS OVER THE LAZ
THE QUICK BROWN FOX JUMPS OVER THE LAZ

ABCDEFGHIJKLMNOPQRSTUVWXYZ
ABCDEFGHIJKLMNOPQRSTUVWXYZ
1234567890 ,.;:?!%‡$¢&#{()}@©

ABCDEFGHIJKLMNOPQRSTUVWXYZ
ABCDEFGHIJKLMNOPQRSTUVWXYZ
1234567890 ,.;:?!%‡$¢&#{()}@©

ABCDEFGHIJKLMNOPQRSTUVWXYZ
ABCDEFGHIJKLMNOPQRSTUVWXYZ
1234567890 .,;:?!%£$¢&#{()}@©

ABCDEFGHIJKLMNOPQRSTUVWXYZ
ABCDEFGHIJKLMNOPQRSTUVWXYZ
1234567890 .,;:?!%£$¢&#{()}@©

ABCDEFGHIJKLMNOPQRSTUVWXYZ
ABCDEFGHIJKLMNOPQRSTUVWXYZ
1234567890 .,;:?!%£$¢&#{()}@©

ABCDEFGHIJKLMNOPQRSTUVWXYZ
ABCDEFGHIJKLMNOPQRSTUVWXYZ
1234567890 .,;:?!%£$¢&#{()}@©

DF Custard

Regular
Condensed

The quick brown fox jumps over the lazy dog.
THE QUICK BROWN FOX JUMPS OVER THE LAZY DOG.
The quick brown fox jumps over the lazy dog.
THE QUICK BROWN FOX JUMPS OVER THE LAZY DOG.
The quick brown fox jumps over the lazy dog.
THE QUICK BROWN FOX JUMPS OVER THE L

ABCDEFGHIJKLMNOPQRSTUVWXYZ
abcdefghijklmnopqrstuvwxyz
1234567890 .,;:?!%£$¢&$&#{[]}@©

ABCDEFGHIJKLMNOPQRSTUVWXYZ
abcdefghijklmnopqrstuvwxyz
1234567890 .,;:?!%£$¢&$&#{[]}@©

Custard Regular 75pt

Jinx Pixiedust

DF Dauphine

Regular
Alternates
Foliage

THE QUICK BROWN FOX JUMPS OVER THE LAZY DOG.
THE QUICK BROWN FOX JUMPS OVER THE LAZY DOG.

THE QUICK BROWN FOX JUMPS OVER THE LAZY DOG.
THE QUICK BROWN FOX JUMPS OVER THE LAZY DOG.

THE QUICK BROWN FOX JUMPS OVER THE LAZY D
THE QUICK BROWN FOX JUMPS OVER THE

↘ alt m, ↘ alt d.

ABCDEFGHIJKLMNOPQRSTUVWXYZ
ABCDEFGHIJKLMNOPQRSTUVWXYZ
1234567890 ,.,:?!%£$¢&#{()}Ⓐ©

ABCDEFGHIJKLMNOPQRSTUVWXYZ
ABCDEFGHIJKLMNOPQRSTUVWXYZ
1234567890 ,.,:?!%£$¢&#{()}Ⓐ©

ABCDEFGHIJKLMNOPQRSTUVWXYZ
ABCDEFGHIJKLMNOPQRSTUVWXYZ
1234567890 ,.,:?!%£$¢&#{()}Ⓐ©

KEW GREENHOUSE

Dauphine Alternates, Dauphine Foliage and Dauphine Regular 58pt

DF Drexler

Regular

the quick brown fox jumps over the lazy dog.
the quick brown fox jumps over the lazy dog.

the quick brown fox jumps over the lazy dog.
the quick brown fox jumps over the lazy dog.

the quick brown fox jumps over the
the quick brown fox jumps over the

abcdefghijklmnopqrstuvwxyz
1234567890 ,.,:?!¡£$c&#{()}@

fabrication gel

Drexler 73pt

DF Dynasty A

Thin
Thin Italic
Light
Light Italic
Demi Bold
Demi Bold Italic
Heavy
Heavy Italic

The quick brown fox jumps over the lazy dog.
THE QUICK BROWN FOX JUMPS OVER THE LAZY DOG.

The quick brown fox jumps over the lazy dog.
THE QUICK BROWN FOX JUMPS OVER THE LAZY DO

The quick brown fox jumps over the laz
THE QUICK BROWN FOX JUMPS OVER T

ABCDEFGHIJKLMNOPQRSTUVWXYZ
abcdefghijklmnopqrstuvwxyz
1234567890 ,.;:?!%£$¢&Nº{()}@©

ABCDEFGHIJKLMNOPQRSTUVWXYZ
abcdefghijklmnopqrstuvwxyz
1234567890 ,.;:?!%£$¢&Nº{()}@©

ABCDEFGHIJKLMNOPQRSTUVWXYZ
abcdefghijklmnopqrstuvwxyz
1234567890 ,.;:?!%£$¢&Nº{()}@©

ABCDEFGHIJKLMNOPQRSTUVWXYZ
abcdefghijklmnopqrstuvwxyz
1234567890 ,.;:?!%£$¢&Nº{()}@©

ABCDEFGHIJKLMNOPQRSTUVWXYZ
abcdefghijklmnopqrstuvwxyz
1234567890 ,.;:?!%£$¢&Nº{()}@©

ABCDEFGHIJKLMNOPQRSTUVWXYZ
abcdefghijklmnopqrstuvwxyz
1234567890 ,.;:?!%£$¢&Nº{()}@©

ABCDEFGHIJKLMNOPQRSTUVWXYZ
abcdefghijklmnopqrstuvwxyz
1234567890 ,.;:?!%£$¢&Nº{()}@©

ABCDEFGHIJKLMNOPQRSTUVWXYZ
abcdefghijklmnopqrstuvwxyz
1234567890 ,.;:?!%£$¢&N°{()}@©

DF Dynasty B

Extra Light
Extra Light Italic
Medium
Medium Italic
Bold
Bold Italic

The quick brown fox jumps over the lazy dog.
THE QUICK BROWN FOX JUMPS OVER THE LAZY DOG.

The quick brown fox jumps over the lazy dog.
THE QUICK BROWN FOX JUMPS OVER THE LAZY DOG.

The quick brown fox jumps over the la
THE QUICK BROWN FOX JUMPS OVER

ABCDEFGHIJKLMNOPQRSTUVWXYZ
abcdefghijklmnopqrstuvwxyz
1234567890 ,.;:?!%£$¢&N°{()}@©

ABCDEFGHIJKLMNOPQRSTUVWXYZ
abcdefghijklmnopqrstuvwxyz
1234567890 ,.;:?!%£$¢&N°{()}@©

ABCDEFGHIJKLMNOPQRSTUVWXYZ
abcdefghijklmnopqrstuvwxyz
1234567890 ,.;:?!%£$¢&N°{()}@©

ABCDEFGHIJKLMNOPQRSTUVWXYZ
abcdefghijklmnopqrstuvwxyz
1234567890 ,.;:?!%£$¢&N°{()}@©

ABCDEFGHIJKLMNOPQRSTUVWXYZ
abcdefghijklmnopqrstuvwxyz
1234567890 ,.;:?!%£$¢&N°{()}@©

ABCDEFGHIJKLMNOPQRSTUVWXYZ
abcdefghijklmnopqrstuvwxyz
1234567890 ,.;:?!%£$¢&N°{()}@©

DF Egret

Light
Light Flourish

The quick brown fox jumps over the lazy dog
THE QUICK BROWN FOX JUMPS OVER THE LAZY DOG

The quick brown fox jumps over the lazy dog
THE QUICK BROWN FOX JUMPS OVER THE LAZY DOG

The quick brown fox jumps over the lo
THE QUICK BROWN FOX JUMPS OVER

ABCDEFGHIJKLMNOPQRSTUVWXYZ
abcdefghijklmnopqrstuvwxyz
1234567890 ,.;:?!%£$¢ʁ#{()}@©

ABCDEFGHIJKLMNOPQRSTUVWXYZ
abcdefghijklmnopqrstuvwxyz
1234567890 ,.;:?!%£$¢ʁ#{()}@©

Coronation

Egret Light Flourish 75pt

DF Electrasonic

XX Fine
X Fine
Fine

ᴜ alt w

The quick brown fox jumps over the lazy dog.
The Quick Brown Fox Jumps Over The Lazy Dog.

The quick brown fox jumps over the lazy dog.
The Quick Brown Fox Jumps Over The Lazy Dog

The quick brown fox jumps over the lazy do
The Quick Brown Fox Jumps Over The

ABCDEFGHIJKLMNOPQRST
UVWXYZ abcdefghijklmnopqrstuvwxyz
1234567890 ,.;:?!%£$¢ʁ#[()]@©

ABCDEFGHIJKLMNOPQRST
UVWXYZ abcdefghijklmnopqrstuvwxyz
1234567890 ,.;:?!%£$¢ʁ#[()]@©

ABCDEFGHIJKLMNOPQRST
UVWXYZ abcdefghijklmnopqrstuvwxyz
1234567890 ,.;:?!%£$¢ʁ#[()]@©

DF Galaxie

Light
Light Italic
Medium
Medium Italic
Bold
Bold Italic

The quick brown fox jumps over the lazy dog.
THE QUICK BROWN FOX JUMPS OVER THE LAZY DOG.

The quick brown fox jumps over the lazy dog.
THE QUICK BROWN FOX JUMPS OVER THE L

The quick brown fox jumps over
THE QUICK BROWN FOX JUMPS

ABCDEFGHIJKLMNOPQRSTUVWXYZ
abcdefghijklmnopqrstuvwxyz
1234567890 ,.;:?!%£$¢&#{[]}@©

ABCDEFGHIJKLMNOPQRSTUVWXYZ
abcdefghijklmnopqrstuvwxyz
1234567890 ,.;:?!%£$¢&#{[]}@©

ABCDEFGHIJKLMNOPQRSTUVWXYZ
abcdefghijklmnopqrstuvwxyz
1234567890 ,.;:?!%£$¢&#{[]}@©

ABCDEFGHIJKLMNOPQRSTUVWXYZ
abcdefghijklmnopqrstuvwxyz
1234567890 ,.;:?!%£$¢&#{[]}@©

ABCDEFGHIJKLMNOPQRSTUVWXYZ
abcdefghijklmnopqrstuvwxyz
1234567890 ,.;:?!%£$¢&#{[]}@©

ABCDEFGHIJKLMNOPQRSTUVWXYZ
abcdefghijklmnopqrstuvwxyz
1234567890 ,.;:?!%£$¢&#{[]}@©

Rekyavik

Galaxie Bold 58pt

DF Galicia

Light
Light Italic
Medium
Medium Italic

The quick brown fox jumps over the lazy dog.
THE QUICK BROWN FOX JUMPS OVER THE LAZY DOG.

The quick brown fox jumps over the lazy dog.
THE QUICK BROWN FOX JUMPS OVER THE LAZY

The quick brown fox jumps over the la
THE QUICK BROWN FOX JUMPS OVE

ABCDEFGHIJKLMNOPQRSTUVWXYZ
abcdefghijklmnopqrstuvwxyz
1234567890 ,.;:?!%£¢$&#-[()]-@©

ABCDEFGHIJKLMNOPQRSTUVWXYZ
abcdefghijklmnopqrstuvwxyz
1234567890 ,.;:?!%£¢$&#-[()]-@©

ABCDEFGHIJKLMNOPQRSTUVWXYZ
abcdefghijklmnopqrstuvwxyz
1234567890 ,.;:?!%£¢$&#-[()]-@©

ABCDEFGHIJKLMNOPQRSTUVWXYZ
abcdefghijklmnopqrstuvwxyz
1234567890 ,.;:?!%£¢$&#-[()]-@©

DF Gentry

Medium
Bold

The quick brown fox jumps over the lazy dog.
THE QUICK BROWN FOX JUMPS OVER THE LAZY DOG.

The quick brown fox jumps over the lazy dog.
THE QUICK BROWN FOX JUMPS OVER THE LAZY DOG.

The quick brown fox jumps over the lazy d
THE QUICK BROWN FOX JUMPS OVER T

ABCDEFGHIJKLMNOPQRSTUVWXYZ
abcdefghijklmnopqrstuvwxyz
1234567890 ,.;:?!%£ş¿&#[[]]@©

ABCDEFGHIJKLMNOPQRSTUVWXYZ
abcdefghijklmnopqrstuvwxyz
1234567890 ,.;:?!%£ş¿&#[[]]@©

DF Glitterati

Light
Alternates

The quick brown fox jumps over the lazy dog.
THE QUICK BROWN FOX JUMPS OVER THE LAZY DOG.

The quick brown fox jumps over the lazy dog.
THE QUICK BROWN FOX JUMPS OVER THE LAZY DOG.

The quick brown fox jumps over the lazy d
THE QUICK BROWN FOX JUMPS OVER THE LA

ABCDEFGHIJKLMNOPQRSTUVWXYZ
abcdefghijklmnopqrstuvwxyz
1234567890 ,.;:?!%£$¢&#{()}@©

ABCDEFGHIJKLMNOPQRSTUVWXYZ OOFOTTOO
abcdefghijklmnopqrstuvwxyz ebfnerssootuttoo
1234567890 ,.;:?!%£$¢&'#{()}@© Alternates contains
kerned ligatures (not all shown)

DF Gridlocker

One
Two

THE QUICK BROWN FOX JUMPS
OVER THE LAZY DOG!
THE QUICK BROWN FOX JUMPS
OVER THE LAZY DOG!
THE QUICK BROWN FOX
JUMPS OVER THE LAZY DOG.

ABCDEFGHIJKLMNOPQR
STUVWXYZ1234567890
,.!.!?!%£$¢&#[[]]@

ABCDEFGHIJKLMNOPQR
STUVWXYZ1234567890
,.!.!?!%£$¢&#////@

DF Gusto

Regular
Solid
Highlight

THE QUICK BROWN FOX JUMPS OVER THE LAZY DOG.
THE QUICK BROWN FOX JUMPS OVER THE LAZY DOG.

THE QUICK BROWN FOX JUMPS OVER THE LAZY DOG.
THE QUICK BROWN FOX JUMPS OVER THE LAZY DOG.

THE QUICK BROWN FOX JUMPS
THE QUICK BROWN FOX JUMPS

ABCDEFGHIJKLMNOPQRSTUVWXYZ
ABCDEFGHIJKLMNOPQRSTUVWXYZ
18 48~ 8° ,.;: !!%&° 8°° () ©©

ABCDEFGHIJKLMNOPQRSTUVWXYZ
ABCDEFGHIJKLMNOPQRSTUVWXYZ
1234567890 ,.·;:?!%£$¢§#°‹()›△©

ABCDEFGHIJKLMNOPQRSTUVWXYZ
ABCDEFGHIJKLMNOPQRSTUVWXYZ
1234567890 ,.·;:?!%£$¢§#°‹()›△©

BLIMP!

Gusto Regular 84pt

DF Interceptor

Regular
Regular Italic
Nitro
Nitro Italic

THE QUICK BROWN FOX JUMPS OVER THE LAZY DOG.
THE QUICK BROWN FOX JUMPS OVER THE LAZY DOG.

THE QUICK BROWN FOX JUMPS OVER THE
THE QUICK BROWN FOX JUMPS OVER THE

THE QUICK BROWN FOX JUMPS
THE QUICK BROWN FOX JUMPS

ABCDEFGHIJKLMNOPQRS
TUVWXYZ 1234567890
,.·;:?!%£$¢§#{()}△©

ABCDEFGHIJKLMNOPQRS
TUVWXYZ 1234567890
,.·;:?!%£$¢§#{()}△©

ABCDEFGHIJKLMNOPQRS
TUVWXYZ 1234567890
,.·;:?!%£$¢§#{()}△©

ABCDEFGHIJKLMNOPQRS
TUVWXYZ 1234567890
,.·;:?!%£$¢§#{()}△©

DF Ministry A

Thin
Thin Italic
Light
Light Italic
Bold
Bold Italic
Heavy
Heavy Italic

The quick brown fox jumps over the lazy dog.
THE QUICK BROWN FOX JUMPS OVER THE LAZY DOG.
The quick brown fox jumps over the lazy dog.
THE QUICK BROWN FOX JUMPS OVER THE LAZY DO
The quick brown fox jumps over the l
THE QUICK BROWN FOX JUMPS OVE

ABCDEFGHIJKLMNOPQRSTUVWXYZ
abcdefghijklmnopqrstuvwxyz
1234567890 ,.;:?!%£$¢&#{[]}@©

ABCDEFGHIJKLMNOPQRSTUVWXYZ
abcdefghijklmnopqrstuvwxyz
1234567890 ,.;:?!%£$¢&#{[]}@©

ABCDEFGHIJKLMNOPQRSTUVWXYZ
abcdefghijklmnopqrstuvwxyz
1234567890 ,.;:?!%£$¢&#{[]}@©

ABCDEFGHIJKLMNOPQRSTUVWXYZ
abcdefghijklmnopqrstuvwxyz
1234567890 ,.;:?!%£$¢&#{[]}@©

ABCDEFGHIJKLMNOPQRSTUVWXYZ
abcdefghijklmnopqrstuvwxyz
1234567890 ,.;:?!%£$¢&#{[]}@©

ABCDEFGHIJKLMNOPQRSTUVWXYZ
abcdefghijklmnopqrstuvwxyz
1234567890 ,.;:?!%£$¢&#{[]}@©

ABCDEFGHIJKLMNOPQRSTUVWXYZ
abcdefghijklmnopqrstuvwxyz
1234567890 ,.;:?!%£$¢&#{[]}@©

ABCDEFGHIJKLMNOPQRSTUVWXYZ
abcdefghijklmnopqrstuvwxyz
1234567890 ,.;:?!%£$¢&#{[]}@©

DF Ministry B

Extra Light
Extra Light Italic
Medium
Medium Italic
Extra Bold
Extra Bold Italic

Eal

The quick brown fox jumps over the lazy dog.
THE QUICK BROWN FOX JUMPS OVER THE LAZY DOG.
The quick brown fox jumps over the lazy dog.
THE QUICK BROWN FOX JUMPS OVER THE LAZY
The quick brown fox jumps over the l
THE QUICK BROWN FOX JUMPS OVE

ABCDEFGHIJKLMNOPQRSTUVWXYZ
abcdefghijklmnopqrstuvwxyz
1234567890 ,.;:?!%£$¢&#{[]}@©

ABCDEFGHIJKLMNOPQRSTUVWXYZ
abcdefghijklmnopqrstuvwxyz
1234567890 ,.;:?!%£$¢&#{[]}@©

ABCDEFGHIJKLMNOPQRSTUVWXYZ
abcdefghijklmnopqrstuvwxyz
1234567890 ,.;:?!%£$¢&#{[]}@©

ABCDEFGHIJKLMNOPQRSTUVWXYZ
abcdefghijklmnopqrstuvwxyz
1234567890 ,.;:?!%£$¢&#{[]}@©

ABCDEFGHIJKLMNOPQRSTUVWXYZ
abcdefghijklmnopqrstuvwxyz
1234567890 ,.;:?!%£$¢&#{[]}@©

ABCDEFGHIJKLMNOPQRSTUVWXYZ
abcdefghijklmnopqrstuvwxyz
1234567890 ,.;:?!%£$¢&#{[]}@©

DF Miserichordia

Regular
Alternatives

Eal

The quick brown fox jumps over the lazy dog.
THE QUICK BROWN FOX JUMPS OVER THE LAZY DOG.

The quick brown fox jumps over the lazy dog.
THE QUICK BROWN FOX JUMPS OVER THE LAZY DOG.

The quick brown fox jumps over the lazy dog.
THE QUICK BROWN FOX JUMPS OVER THE LAZY DOG.

ABCDEFGHIJKLMNOPQRSTUVWXYZ 1234567890
abcdefghijklmnopqrstuvwxyz ,.:;?!%£$¢&№{()}@©

ABCDEFGHIJKLMNOPQRSTUVWXYZ 1234567890
abcdefghijklmnopqrstuvwxyz ,.:;?!%£$¢&№{()}@©

DF Monitor

Regular

THE QUICK BROWN FOX JUMPS OVER THE LAZY DOG.
THE QUICK BROWN FOX JUMPS OVER THE LAZY DOG.

THE QUICK BROWN FOX JUMPS OVER
THE QUICK BROWN FOX JUMPS OVER

THE QUICK BROWN FOX JU
THE QUICK BROWN FOX JU

ABCDEFGHIJKLMNOPQRS
TUVWXYZ 1234567890
.,.:;?!%£$¢&№*()}@©

DF Moonstone

Regular
Starlight

Eal

f alt d

The quick brown fox jumps over the lazy dog.
THE QUICK BROWN FOX JUMPS OVER THE LAZY DOG.

The quick brown fox jumps over the lazy dog.
THE QUICK BROWN FOX JUMPS OVER THE LAZY DOG.

The quick brown fox jumps over the lazy dog.
THE QUICK BROWN FOX JUMPS OVER THE LAZY DOG.

ABCDEFGHIJKLMNOPQRSTUVWXYZ 1234567890
abcdefghijklmnopqrstuvwxyz ,.+:?!%£$¢#()}@©

ABCDEFGHIJKLMNOPQRSTUVWXYZ 1234567890
abcdefghijklmnopqrstuvwxyz ,+.+:?!%£$¢#()}@©

DF Mulgrave

Regular

THE QUICK BROWN FOX JUMPS OVER THE LAZY DOG.
THE QUICK BROWN FOX JUMPS OVER THE LAZY DOG.
THE QUICK BROWN FOX JUMPS OVER THE LA
THE QUICK BROWN FOX JUMPS OVER THE LA
THE QUICK BROWN FOX JUMPS OVER
THE QUICK BROWN FOX JUMPS OVER

ABCDEFGHIJKLMNOPQRSTUVWXYZ
ABCDEFGHIJKLMNOPQRSTUVWXYZ
1234567890 ,.;:?!%£$¢&#{[]}@©

DF Outlander Nova
Light
Light Italic
Medium
Medium Italic
Bold
Bold Italic
Black
Black Italic

THE QUICK BROWN FOX JUMPS OVER THE LAZY DOG.
THE QUICK BROWN FOX JUMPS OVER THE LAZY DOG.
THE QUICK BROWN FOX JUMPS OVER
THE QUICK BROWN FOX JUMPS OVER
THE QUICK BROWN FOX JUMP
THE QUICK BROWN FOX JUMP

ABCDEFGHIJKLMNOPQRSTUVWXYZ
ABCDEFGHIJKLMNOPQRSTUVWXYZ
1234567890 ,.;:?!%£$¢&#{()}@©

ABCDEFGHIJKLMNOPQRSTUVWXYZ
ABCDEFGHIJKLMNOPQRSTUVWXYZ
1234567890 ,.;:?!%£$¢&#{()}@©

ABCDEFGHIJKLMNOPQRSTUVWXYZ
ABCDEFGHIJKLMNOPQRSTUVWXYZ
1234567890 ,.;:?!%£$¢&#{()}@©

ABCDEFGHIJKLMNOPQRSTUVWXYZ
ABCDEFGHIJKLMNOPQRSTUVWXYZ
1234567890 ,.;:?!%£$¢&#{()}@©

ABCDEFGHIJKLMNOPQRSTUVWXYZ
ABCDEFGHIJKLMNOPQRSTUVWXYZ
1234567890 ,.;:?!%£$¢&#{()}@©

ABCDEFGHIJKLMNOPQRSTUVWXYZ
ABCDEFGHIJKLMNOPQRSTUVWXYZ
1234567890 ,.;:?!%£$¢&#(()}ⓐⓒ

ABCDEFGHIJKLMNOPQRSTUVWXYZ
ABCDEFGHIJKLMNOPQRSTUVWXYZ
1234567890 ,.;:?!%£$¢&#(()}ⓐⓒ

ABCDEFGHIJKLMNOPQRSTUVWXYZ
ABCDEFGHIJKLMNOPQRSTUVWXYZ
1234567890 ,.;:?!%£$¢&#(()}ⓐⓒ

DF Payload

Regular
Outline
Spraycan

EA1

THE QUICK BROWN FOX JUMPS OVER THE LAZY DOG.
THE QUICK BROWN FOX JUMPS OVER THE LAZY DOG.

THE QUICK BROWN FOX JUMPS OVER THE
THE QUICK BROWN FOX JUMPS OVER THE

THE QUICK BROWN FOX JUMP
THE QUICK BROWN FOX JUMP

ABCDEFGHIJKLMNOPQRSTUVWXYZ
ABCDEFGHIJKLMNOPQRSTUVWXYZ
1234567890 ,.;:?!%£$¢&№?((),)ⓒ

ABCDEFGHIJKLMNOPQRSTUVWXYZ
ABCDEFGHIJKLMNOPQRSTUVWXYZ
1234567890 ,.;:?!%£$¢&№?(()})ⓒ

ABCDEFGHIJKLMNOPQRSTUVWXYZ
ABCDEFGHIJKLMNOPQRSTUVWXYZ
1234567890 ,.;:?!%£$¢&№?(()})ⓒ

ENGINE 2

Payload Spraycan 67pt

DF Payload Narrow

Regular
Outline

THE QUICK BROWN FOX JUMPS OVER THE LAZY DOG.
THE QUICK BROWN FOX JUMPS OVER THE LAZY DOG.

THE QUICK BROWN FOX JUMPS OVER THE LAZY DOG.
THE QUICK BROWN FOX JUMPS OVER THE LAZY DOG.

THE QUICK BROWN FOX JUMPS OVER THE LAZY DO
THE QUICK BROWN FOX JUMPS OVER THE LAZY DO

ABCDEFGHIJKLMNOPQRSTUVWXYZ
ABCDEFGHIJKLMNOPQRSTUVWXYZ
1234567890 ,.;:?!%£$€GN°!([])@@

ABCDEFGHIJKLMNOPQRSTUVWXYZ
ABCDEFGHIJKLMNOPQRSTUVWXYZ
1234567890 ,.;:?!%£$€GN°!([])@@

WARZONE

Payload Narrow, Payload Wide and Payload Wide Ouline 60pt

DF Payload Wide

Regular
Outline

THE QUICK BROWN FOX
JUMPS OVER THE LAZY DOG.

THE QUICK BROWN FOX
JUMPS OVER THE LAZY

THE QUICK BROWN
JUMPS OVER THE L

ABCDEFGHIJKLMNOPQRSTU
VWXYZABCDEFGHIJKLMNOP
QRSTUVWXYZ1234567890
,.;:?!%£$€GN°!([])@@

ABCDEFGHIJKLMNOPQRSTU
VWXYZABCDEFGHIJKLMNOP
QRSTUVWXYZ1234567890
,.;:?!%£$€GN°!([])@@

Clement La FRAISE

Pitshanger and Pitshanger Initial Capitals 57pt

DF Pitshanger

Regular
Initial Capitals

The quick brown fox jumps over the lazy dog.
THE QUICK BROWN FOX JUMPS OVER THE LAZY DOG.

The quick brown fox jumps over the lazy dog.
THE QUICK BROWN FOX JUMPS OVER THE LAZY DOG.

The quick brown fox jumps over the lazy dog.
THE QUICK BROWN FOX JUMPS OVER THE LAZY

E alt d, F alt w, ✧ alt 8

ABCDEFGHIJKLMNOPQRSTUVWXYZ 1234567890
abcdefghijklmnopqrstuvwxyz ,.;:?!%£$¢&№·{|}

ABCDEFGHIJKLMNOPQRSTUVWXYZ 1234567890
ABCDEFGHIJKLMNOPQRSTUVWXYZ ,.;:?!%£$¢&№·{|}

DF Radiogram

Regular
Tall
Solid Regular
Solid Tall

The quick brown fox jumps over the lazy dog.
THE QUICK BROWN FOX JUMPS OVER THE LAZY DOG.

The quick brown fox jumps over the lazy dog.
THE QUICK BROWN FOX JUMPS OVER THE LAZY DOG.

The quick brown fox jumps over the lazy dog.
THE QUICK BROWN FOX JUMPS OVER THE LAZY DOG.

ABCDEFGHIJKLMNOPQRSTUVWXYZ 1234567890
abcdefghijklmnopqrstuvwxyz ,.;:?!%£$¢&#{()}

ABCDEFGHIJKLMNOPQRSTUVWXYZ 1234567890
abcdefghijklmnopqrstuvwxyz ,.;:?!%£$¢&#{()}

ABCDEFGHIJKLMNOPQRSTUVWXYZ 1234567890
abcdefghijklmnopqrstuvwxyz ,.;:?!%£$¢&#{()}

ABCDEFGHIJKLMNOPQRSTUVWXYZ 1234567890
abcdefghijklmnopqrstuvwxyz ,.;:?!%£$¢&#{()}

DF Ritafurey A

Extra Light
Extra Light Italic
Medium
Medium Italic
Bold
Bold Italic

The quick brown fox jumps over the lazy dog.
THE QUICK BROWN FOX JUMPS OVER THE LAZY DOG.

The quick brown fox jumps over the lazy dog
THE QUICK BROWN FOX JUMPS OVER THE

The quick brown fox jumps over t
THE QUICK BROWN FOX JUMPS

ABCDEFGHIJKLMNOPQRSTUVWXYZ
abcdefghijklmnopqrstuvwxyz
1234567890 ,.;:?!%£$¢&#{()}@©

ABCDEFGHIJKLMNOPQRSTUVWXYZ
abcdefghijklmnopqrstuvwxyz
1234567890 ,.;:?!%£$¢&#{()}@©

Transfixed

Ritafurey Extra Light 76pt

ABCDEFGHIJKLMNOPQRSTUVWXYZ
abcdefghijklmnopqrstuvwxyz
1234567890 ,.;:?!%£$¢&#{()}@©

ABCDEFGHIJKLMNOPQRSTUVWXYZ
abcdefghijklmnopqrstuvwxyz
1234567890 ,.;:?!%£$¢&#{()}@©

ABCDEFGHIJKLMNOPQRSTUVWXYZ
abcdefghijklmnopqrstuvwxyz
1234567890 ,.;:?!%£$¢&#{()}@©

ABCDEFGHIJKLMNOPQRSTUVWXYZ
abcdefghijklmnopqrstuvwxyz
1234567890 ,.;:?!%£$¢&#{()}@©

DF Ritafurey B

Thin
Thin Italic
Light
Light Italic
Demi Bold
Demi Bold Italic

The quick brown fox jumps over the lazy dog.
THE QUICK BROWN FOX JUMPS OVER THE LAZY DOG.
The quick brown fox jumps over the lazy dog
THE QUICK BROWN FOX JUMPS OVER THE
The quick brown fox jumps over t
THE QUICK BROWN FOX JUMPS

ABCDEFGHIJKLMNOPQRSTUVWXYZ
abcdefghijklmnopqrstuvwxyz
1234567890 ,.;:?!%£$¢&#{()}@©

ABCDEFGHIJKLMNOPQRSTUVWXYZ
abcdefghijklmnopqrstuvwxyz
1234567890 ,.;:?!%£$¢&#{()}@©

ABCDEFGHIJKLMNOPQRSTUVWXYZ
abcdefghijklmnopqrstuvwxyz
1234567890 ,.;:?!%£$¢&#{()}@©

ABCDEFGHIJKLMNOPQRSTUVWXYZ
abcdefghijklmnopqrstuvwxyz
1234567890 ,.;:?!%£$¢&#{()}@©

ABCDEFGHIJKLMNOPQRSTUVWXYZ
abcdefghijklmnopqrstuvwxyz
1234567890 ,.;:?!%£$¢&#{()}@©

ABCDEFGHIJKLMNOPQRSTUVWXYZ
abcdefghijklmnopqrstuvwxyz
1234567890 ,.;:?!%£$¢&#{()}@©

Ritafurey Demi Bold Italic 83pt

DF Roadkill

Regular

EA1

THE QUICK BROWN FOX JUMPS OVER THE LAZY DOG.
THE QUICK BROWN FOX JUMPS OVER THE LAZY DOG.
THE QUICK BROWN FOX JUMPS OVER THE LAZY DOG.
THE QUICK BROWN FOX JUMPS OVER THE LAZY DOG.
THE QUICK BROWN FOX JUMPS OVER THE LAZY DOG.
THE QUICK BROWN FOX JUMPS OVER THE LAZY DOG.

ABCDEFGHIJKLMNOPQRSTUVWXYZABCDEFGHIJKLMN
OPQRSTUVWXYZ 1234567890 ,.;:?!%£$¢&#{[]}@

DF Rogue Sans

Light
Light Italic
Medium
Medium Italic
Bold
Bold Italic

The quick brown fox jumps over the lazy dog.
THE QUICK BROWN FOX JUMPS OVER THE LAZY DOG.

The quick brown fox jumps over the lazy dog.
THE QUICK BROWN FOX JUMPS OVER THE LAZY DOG.

The quick brown fox jumps over the lazy dog.
THE QUICK BROWN FOX JUMPS OVER THE LAZY D

ABCDEFGHIJKLMNOPQRSTUVWXYZ
abcdefghijklmnopqrstuvwxyz
1234567890 ,.;:?!%£$¢&#(0)@©

ABCDEFGHIJKLMNOPQRSTUVWXYZ
abcdefghijklmnopqrstuvwxyz
1234567890 ,.;:?!%£$¢&#(0)@©

ABCDEFGHIJKLMNOPQRSTUVWXYZ
abcdefghijklmnopqrstuvwxyz
1234567890 ,.;:?!%£$¢&#(0)@©

ABCDEFGHIJKLMNOPQRSTUVWXYZ
abcdefghijklmnopqrstuvwxyz
1234567890 ,.;:?!%£$¢&#(0)@©

ABCDEFGHIJKLMNOPQRSTUVWXYZ
abcdefghijklmnopqrstuvwxyz
1234567890 ,.;:?!%£$¢&#(0)@©

ABCDEFGHIJKLMNOPQRSTUVWXYZ
abcdefghijklmnopqrstuvwxyz
1234567890 ,.;:?!%£$¢&#(()}@©

**DF Rogue Sans
Condensed**

Light
Light Italic
Medium
Medium Italic
Bold
Bold Italic

The quick brown fox jumps over the lazy dog.
THE QUICK BROWN FOX JUMPS OVER THE LAZY DOG.
The quick brown fox jumps over the lazy dog.
THE QUICK BROWN FOX JUMPS OVER THE LAZY DOG.
The quick brown fox jumps over the lazy dog.
THE QUICK BROWN FOX JUMPS OVER THE LAZY DOG.

ABCDEFGHIJKLMNOPQRSTUVWXYZ
abcdefghijklmnopqrstuvwxyz
1234567890 ,.;:?!%£$¢&#(()}@©

ABCDEFGHIJKLMNOPQRSTUVWXYZ
abcdefghijklmnopqrstuvwxyz
1234567890 ,.;:?!%£$¢&#(()}@©

ABCDEFGHIJKLMNOPQRSTUVWXYZ
abcdefghijklmnopqrstuvwxyz
1234567890 ,.;:?!%£$¢&#(()}@©

ABCDEFGHIJKLMNOPQRSTUVWXYZ
abcdefghijklmnopqrstuvwxyz
1234567890 ,.;:?!%£$¢&#(()}@©

ABCDEFGHIJKLMNOPQRSTUVWXYZ
abcdefghijklmnopqrstuvwxyz
1234567890 ,.;:?!%£$¢&#(()}@©

ABCDEFGHIJKLMNOPQRSTUVWXYZ
abcdefghijklmnopqrstuvwxyz
1234567890 ,.;:?!%£$¢&#(()}@©

DF Rogue Sans Extended

Light
Light Italic
Medium
Medium Italic
Bold
Bold Italic

The quick brown fox jumps over the lazy dog.
THE QUICK BROWN FOX JUMPS OVER THE LAZY DOG.

The quick brown fox jumps over the lazy dog.
THE QUICK BROWN FOX JUMPS OVER THE LAZY DO

The quick brown fox jumps over the
THE QUICK BROWN FOX JUMPS OVER

ABCDEFGHIJKLMNOPQRSTUVWXYZ
abcdefghijklmnopqrstuvwxyz
1234567890 ,.;:?!%£$¢&#{()}@©

ABCDEFGHIJKLMNOPQRSTUVWXYZ
abcdefghijklmnopqrstuvwxyz
1234567890 ,.;:?!%£$¢&#{()}@©

Architecture

Rogue Sans Extended Light 56pt

ABCDEFGHIJKLMNOPQRSTUVWXYZ
abcdefghijklmnopqrstuvwxyz
1234567890 ,.;:?!%£$¢&#{()}@©

ABCDEFGHIJKLMNOPQRSTUVWXYZ
abcdefghijklmnopqrstuvwxyz
1234567890 ,.;:?!%£$¢&#{()}@©

ABCDEFGHIJKLMNOPQRSTUVWXYZ
abcdefghijklmnopqrstuvwxyz
1234567890 ,.;:?!%£$¢&#{()}@©

ABCDEFGHIJKLMNOPQRSTUVWXYZ
abcdefghijklmnopqrstuvwxyz
1234567890 ,.;:?!%£$¢&#{()}@©

DF Rogue Serif

Light
Light Italic
Medium
Medium Italic
Bold
Bold Italic

The quick brown fox jumps over the lazy dog.
THE QUICK BROWN FOX JUMPS OVER THE LAZY DOG.
The quick brown fox jumps over the lazy dog.
THE QUICK BROWN FOX JUMPS OVER THE LAZY DOG.
The quick brown fox jumps over the lazy
THE QUICK BROWN FOX JUMPS OVER THE

ABCDEFGHIJKLMNOPQRSTUVWXYZ
abcdefghijklmnopqrstuvwxyz
1234567890 ,.;:?!%£$¢&#{()}@©

ABCDEFGHIJKLMNOPQRSTUVWXYZ
abcdefghijklmnopqrstuvwxyz
1234567890 ,.;:?!%£$¢&#{()}@©

ABCDEFGHIJKLMNOPQRSTUVWXYZ
abcdefghijklmnopqrstuvwxyz
1234567890 ,.;:?!%£$¢&#{()}@©

ABCDEFGHIJKLMNOPQRSTUVWXYZ
abcdefghijklmnopqrstuvwxyz
1234567890 ,.;:?!%£$¢&#{()}@©

ABCDEFGHIJKLMNOPQRSTUVWXYZ
abcdefghijklmnopqrstuvwxyz
1234567890 ,.;:?!%£$¢&#{()}@©

ABCDEFGHIJKLMNOPQRSTUVWXYZ
abcdefghijklmnopqrstuvwxyz
1234567890 ,.;:?!%£$¢&#{()}@©

Inter*National*

Rogue Serif Light and Bold Italic 62pt

DF September

Medium
Medium Italic
Bold
Bold Italic
Heavy
Heavy Italic

The quick brown fox jumps over the lazy dog.
THE QUICK BROWN FOX JUMPS OVER THE LAZY DOG.

The quick brown fox jumps over the lazy dog.
THE QUICK BROWN FOX JUMPS OVER THE LAZY DOG.

The quick brown fox jumps over the lazy dog.
THE QUICK BROWN FOX JUMPS OVER THE LA

ABCDEFGHIJKLMNOPQRSTUVWXYZ
abcdefghijklmnopqrstuvwxyz
1234567890 ,.;:?!%£$¢&#{()}@©

ABCDEFGHIJKLMNOPQRSTUVWXYZ
abcdefghijklmnopqrstuvwxyz
1234567890 ,.;:?!%£$¢&#{()}@©

ABCDEFGHIJKLMNOPQRSTUVWXYZ
abcdefghijklmnopqrstuvwxyz
1234567890 ,.;:?!%£$¢&#{()}@©

ABCDEFGHIJKLMNOPQRSTUVWXYZ
abcdefghijklmnopqrstuvwxyz
1234567890 ,.;:?!%£$¢&#{()}@©

ABCDEFGHIJKLMNOPQRSTUVWXYZ
abcdefghijklmnopqrstuvwxyz
1234567890 ,.;:?!%£$¢&#{()}@©

ABCDEFGHIJKLMNOPQRSTUVWXYZ
abcdefghijklmnopqrstuvwxyz
1234567890 ,.;:?!%£$¢&#{()}@©

360 degrees

September Heavy and September Medium 74pt

DF Sparrowhawk

Regular

THE QUICK BROWN FOX JUMPS OVER THE LAZY DOG.
THE QUICK BROWN FOX JUMPS OVER THE LAZY DOG.

THE QUICK BROWN FOX JUMPS OVER THE LAZY DO
THE QUICK BROWN FOX JUMPS OVER THE LAZY DO

THE QUICK BROWN FOX JUMPS OVER TH
THE QUICK BROWN FOX JUMPS OVER TH

ABCDEFGHIJKLMNOPQR
STUVWXYZ 1234567890
,.:;?!%£$¢&#{()}Ⓐ©

DF Straker

Regular

The quick brown fox jumps over the lazy dog.   a alt m, e alt d, G alt w
THE QUICK BROWN FOX JUMPS OVER THE LAZY DOG.

The quick brown fox jumps over the lazy dog.
THE QUICK BROWN FOX JUMPS OVER THE LAZY DOG.

The quick brown fox jumps over the lazy
THE QUICK BROWN FOX JUMPS OVER THE LAZ

ABCDEFGHIJKLMNOPQRSTUVWXYZ
abcdefghijklmnopqrstuvwxyz
1234567890 ,.:;?!%£$¢&#{[()]}@©

DF Telstar

Regular

The quick brown fox jumps over the lazy dog.
THE QUICK BROWN FOX JUMPS OVER THE LAZY DOG.

The quick brown fox jumps over the lazy dog.
THE QUICK BROWN FOX JUMPS OVER THE LAZY DOG.

The quick brown fox jumps over the lazy dog.
THE QUICK BROWN FOX JUMPS OVER THE LAZY DOG.

ABCDEFGHIJKLMNOPQRSTUVWXYZ 1234567890
abcdefghijklmnopqrstuvwxyz ,.:;?!%£$¢&#{[()]}

DF Valise Montréal

Regular

The quick brown fox jumps over the lazy dog.
THE QUICK BROWN FOX JUMPS OVER THE LAZY DOG.

The quick brown fox jumps over the lazy dog.
THE QUICK BROWN FOX JUMPS OVER THE LAZY DOG.

The quick brown fox jumps over the lazy dog.
THE QUICK BROWN FOX JUMPS OVER THE LAZY DOG.

ABCDEFGHIJKLMNOPQRSTUVWXYZ 1234567890
abcdefghijklmnopqrstuvwxyz ,.:;?!%£$¢&#{[()]}

DF Xenotype

Regular
Shaded

The quick brown fox jumps over the lazy dog.
THE QUICK BROWN FOX JUMPS OVER THE LAZY DOG.

The quick brown fox jumps over the lazy dog.
THE QUICK BROWN FOX JUMPS OVER THE LAZY DOG.

The quick brown fox jumps over the lazy dog.
THE QUICK BROWN FOX JUMPS OVER THE LAZY DOG.

ABCDEFGHIJKLMNOPQRSTUVWXYZ abcdefghijklmno
pqrstuvwxyz 1234567890 ,.;:?!%£$&Nº(([)}@©

ABCDEFGHIJKLMNOPQRSTUVWXYZ abcdefghijklmno
pqrstuvwxyz 1234567890 ,.;:?!%£$&Nº(([)}@©

**DF Yellow
Perforated**

Regular
Solid

The quick brown fox jumps over the lazy dog.
THE QUICK BROWN FOX JUMPS OVER THE LAZY DOG.

The quick brown fox jumps over the lazy dog.
THE QUICK BROWN FOX JUMPS OVER THE LAZY D

The quick brown fox jumps over the laz
THE QUICK BROWN FOX JUMPS OVER TH

ABCDEFGHIJKLMNOPQRSTUVWXYZ
abcdefghijklmnopqrstuvwxyz
1234567890 ,.;:?!%£$¢&#{([)}@©

ABCDEFGHIJKLMNOPQRSTUVWXYZ
abcdefghijklmnopqrstuvwxyz
1234567890 ,.;:?!%£$¢&#{([)}@©

DF Yolanda

Princess
Duchess
Countess

The quick brown fox jumps over the lazy dog.
THE QUICK BROWN FOX JUMPS OVER THE LAZY DOG.

The quick brown fox jumps over the lazy dog.
THE QUICK BROWN FOX JUMPS OVER THE LAZY D

The quick brown fox jumps over the la
THE QUICK BROWN FOX JUMPS OVE

ABCDEFGHIJKLMNOPQRSTUVWXYZ 1234567890
abcdefghijklmnopqrstuvwxyz ,.;:?!%£ $¢&Nº[()]@

▶ ABCDEFGHIJKLMNOPQRSTUVWXYZ 1234567890
abcdefghijklmnopqrstuvwxyz „;:?!%£$¢&№?·{()}·@

ABCDEFGHIJKLMNOPQRSTUVWXYZ 1234567890
abcdefghijklmnopqrstuvwxyz „;:?!%£$¢&№?·{()}·@

Baron's Court

Yolanda Duchess 77pt

DF Zond Diktat

Medium
Bold

THE QUICK BROWN FOX JUMPS OVER THE LAZY DOG.
THE QUICK BROWN FOX JUMPS OVER THE LAZY DOG.

THE QUICK BROWN FOX JUMPS OVER THE LAZY
THE QUICK BROWN FOX JUMPS OVER THE LAZY

THE QUICK BROWN FOX JUMPS OVER
THE QUICK BROWN FOX JUMPS OVER

ABCDEFGHIJKLMNOPQRSTUVWXYZ
ABCDEFGHIJKLMNOPQRSTUVWXYZ
1234567890 ,.;:?!%£&#{[]}@©

ABCDEFGHIJKLMNOPQRSTUVWXYZ
ABCDEFGHIJKLMNOPQRSTUVWXYZ
1234567890 ,.;:?!%£&#{()}@©

WHITE WASH

Zond
Diktat 70pt

Device Collection the

Miserichordia Regular 60 and 29pt

BRA

English Grotesque Black 247pt

ADJUS

English Grotesque Medium 128pt

ADJUST WHEEL BRAKES BY ADJUSTMENT ON BACKPLATE ONLY. DO NOT INTERFERE WITH LINKAGES (SEE HANDBOOK). &*& Qℚ £*£* J*J*

English Grotesque Thin 10pt *Alternative &: option m. Alternative Q: option 5. Alternative £: option v. Alternative J: option j.*

ADJUST WHEEL BRAKES BY ADJUSTMENT ON BACKPLATE ONLY. DO NOT INTERFERE WITH LINKAGES (SEE HANDBOOK). &*& Qℚ £*£* JJ

English Grotesque Light 12pt *Alternative &: option m. Alternative Q: option 5. Alternative £: option v. Alternative J: option j.*

ADJUST WHEEL BRAKES BY ADJUSTMENT ON BACKPLATE ONLY. DO NOT INTERFERE WITH LINKAGES (SEE HANDBOOK). &*& Qℚ £*£* JJ

English Grotesque Medium 15pt *Alternative &: option m. Alternative Q: option 5. Alternative £: option v. Alternative J: option j.*

ADJUST WHEEL BRAKES BY ADJUSTMENT ON BACKPLATE ONLY. DO NOT INTERFERE WITH LINKAGES (SEE HANDBOOK). &*& Qℚ £*£* JJ

English Grotesque Bold 17pt *Alternative &: option m. Alternative Q: option 5. Alternative £: option v. Alternative J: option j.*

ADJUST WHEEL BRAKES BY ADJUSTMENT ON BACKPLATE ONLY. DO NOT INTERFERE WITH LINKAGES (SEE HANDBOOK).

English Grotesque Extra Bold 19pt

ADJUST WHEEL BRAKES BY ADJUSTMENT ON BACKPLATE ONLY. DO NOT INTERFERE WITH LINKAGES (SEE HANDBOOK).

English Grotesque Black 24pt

AKE
TMENT

Before refitting duct block into the machine, loosen off the blade adjustment screws and then firmly tighten and lock the regulation thumb nut at each end of the duct block.

Before starting machine, see that the duct roller may be easily rotated by means of the lever at the end of the roller.

English Grotesque Medium 8pt

Before refitting duct block into the machine, loosen off the blade adjustment screws, and then firmly tighten and lock the regulation thumb nut at each end of the duct block.

Before starting machine, see that the duct roller may be easily rotated by means of the lever at the end of the roller.

Over-tightening of the blade adjustment screws will result in breakages.

English Grotesque Extra Bold 8pt

CAUTION

English Grotesque Black 60pt

Before refitting duct block into the machine, loosen off the blade adjustment screws and then firmly tighten and lock the regulation thumb nut at each end of the duct block.

Before starting machine, see that the duct roller may be easily rotated by means of the lever at the end of the roller.

English Grotesque Black 8pt

Before refitting duct block into the machine, loosen off the blade adjustment screws, and then firmly tighten and lock the regulation thumb nut at each end of the duct block.

Before starting machine, see that the duct roller may be easily rotated by means of the lever at the end of the roller.

Over-tightening of the blade adjustment screws will result in breakages.

English Grotesque Bold and Light 8pt

Over-tightening of the blade adjustment screws will result in breakages.

English Grotesque Light 24pt and English Grotesque Thin 58pt

fashionista

Paralucent Thin 95pt

Jaw-droppingly gorgeous and terrifyingly talented, this group will redefine the zeitgeist. *Meet the new generation of femme fatales.*

Paralucent Thin and Thin Italic 13pt

Jaw-droppingly gorgeous and terrifyingly talented, this group will redefine the zeitgeist. *Meet the new generation of femme fatales.*

Paralucent Extra Light and Extra Light Italic 13pt

Jaw-droppingly gorgeous and terrifyingly talented, this group will redefine the zeitgeist. *Meet the new generation of femme fatales.*

Paralucent Light and Light Italic 13pt

Jaw-droppingly gorgeous and terrifyingly talented, this group will redefine the zeitgeist. *Meet the new generation of femme fatales.*

Paralucent Medium and Medium Italic 13pt

Jaw-droppingly gorgeous and terrifyingly talented, this group will redefine the zeitgeist. *Meet the new generation of femme fatales.*

Paralucent Demi Bold and Demi Bold Italic 13pt

Jaw-droppingly gorgeous and terrifyingly talented, this group will redefine the zeitgeist. *Meet the new generation of femme fatales.*

Paralucent Bold and Bold Italic 13pt

Jaw-droppingly gorgeous and terrifyingly talented, this group will redefine the zeitgeist. *Meet the new generation of femme fatales.*

Paralucent Heavy and Heavy Italic 13pt

Ravishing beauty

Paralucent Demi Bold 52pt

Infinité Translucent luminous loose powder, £59.99; Blatina Milano eau-de-Nil swimsuit, £189.99; Passionata Endless lip colour, £45.00; Fuscia Vinylite stilettos, £870.00; Maurice Lionel lilac beaded rayon vintage silk dress, £3,770.00; M&S underpants model's own.

Paralucent Light 20pt

Basque

Paralucent Light and Paralucent Heavy 127pt

2005 COLOUR COLLECTION

Paralucent Light and Heavy 31pt

There's a cat in my soup..!

Paralucent Bold 70pt

IS YOUR HIGH-OCTANE LIFESTYLE LEADING TO DEMENTIA? Be of good cheer: "Some, if not all, of these effects are reversible", insists Helmut. "It's okay not to be perfect, as long as no-one knows".

Paralucent Heavy 8pt

IS YOUR HIGH-OCTANE LIFESTYLE LEADING TO DEMENTIA? Be of good cheer: "Some, if not all, of these effects are reversible", insists Helmut. "It's okay not to be perfect, as long as no-one knows".

Paralucent Bold 8pt

IS YOUR HIGH-OCTANE LIFESTYLE LEADING TO DEMENTIA? Be of good cheer: "Some, if not all, of these effects are reversible", insists Helmut. "It's okay not to be perfect, as long as no-one knows".

Paralucent Demi Bold 8pt

IS YOUR HIGH-OCTANE LIFESTYLE LEADING TO DEMENTIA? Be of good cheer: "Some, if not all, of these effects are reversible", insists Helmut. "It's okay not to be perfect, as long as no-one knows".

Paralucent Heavy Italic 8pt

IS YOUR HIGH-OCTANE LIFESTYLE LEADING TO DEMENTIA? Be of good cheer: "Some, if not all, of these effects are reversible", insists Helmut. "It's okay not to be perfect, as long as no-one knows".

Paralucent Bold Italic 8pt

IS YOUR HIGH-OCTANE LIFESTYLE LEADING TO DEMENTIA? Be of good cheer: "Some, if not all, of these effects are reversible", insists Helmut. "It's okay not to be perfect, as long as no-one knows".

Paralucent Demi Bold Italic 8pt

IS YOUR HIGH-OCTANE LIFESTYLE LEADING TO DEMENTIA? Be of good cheer: "Some, if not all, of these effects are reversible", insists Helmut. "It's okay not to be perfect, as long as no-one knows".

Paralucent Medium 8pt

IS YOUR HIGH-OCTANE LIFESTYLE LEADING TO DEMENTIA? Be of good cheer: "Some, if not all, of these effects are reversible", insists Helmut. "It's okay not to be perfect, as long as no-one knows".

Paralucent Light 8pt

IS YOUR HIGH-OCTANE LIFESTYLE LEADING TO DEMENTIA? Be of good cheer: "Some, if not all, of these effects are reversible", insists Helmut. "It's okay not to be perfect, as long as no-one knows".

Paralucent Extra Light 8pt

IS YOUR HIGH-OCTANE LIFESTYLE LEADING TO DEMENTIA? Be of good cheer: "Some, if not all, of these effects are reversible", insists Helmut. "It's okay not to be perfect, as long as no-one knows".

Paralucent Medium Italic 8pt

IS YOUR HIGH-OCTANE LIFESTYLE LEADING TO DEMENTIA? Be of good cheer: "Some, if not all, of these effects are reversible", insists Helmut. "It's okay not to be perfect, as long as no-one knows".

Paralucent Light Italic 8pt

IS YOUR HIGH-OCTANE LIFESTYLE LEADING TO DEMENTIA? Be of good cheer: "Some, if not all, of these effects are reversible", insists Helmut. "It's okay not to be perfect, as long as no-one knows".

Paralucent Extra Light Italic 8pt

IS YOUR HIGH-OCTANE LIFESTYLE LEADING TO DEMENTIA? Be of good cheer: "Some, if not all, of these effects are reversible", insists Helmut. "It's okay not to be perfect, as long as no-one knows".

Paralucent Thin 8pt

IS YOUR HIGH-OCTANE LIFESTYLE LEADING TO DEMENTIA? Be of good cheer: "Some, if not all, of these effects are reversible", insists Helmut. "It's okay not to be perfect, as long as no-one knows".

Paralucent Thin Italic 8pt

Paralucent Thin, Medium and Heavy 177pt

Floral woody freshness, *calm and contentment,* tranquillity and balance, **mind and body**

Paralucent Extra Light, Thin, Light and Medium 34pt

4AM N

Paralucent Condensed Heavy and Light Italic 173pt

LATEST

Paralucent Condensed Heavy 60pt

"He who can dominate London dinner table conversation *can dominate the world*"-Wilde

gg ff aa
True Italics

Paralucent Extra Light and Extra Light Italic 92pt and Light 36pt

PAINTING MYSELF WAVING
GOODBYE, gilt-framed and hung
high, linseed oil and canvas
perfume, dust and linen, dark
wood and sunlight through the
skylight, across the room.

Paralucent Condensed Thin 10pt

PAINTING MYSELF WAVING
GOODBYE, gilt-framed and hung
high, linseed oil and canvas
perfume, dust and linen, dark
wood and sunlight through the
skylight, across the room.

Paralucent Condensed Thin Italic 10pt

PAINTING MYSELF WAVING
GOODBYE, gilt-framed and hung
high, linseed oil and canvas
perfume, dust and linen, dark
wood and sunlight through the
skylight, across the room.

Paralucent Condensed Extra Light 10pt

PAINTING MYSELF WAVING
GOODBYE, gilt-framed and hung
high, linseed oil and canvas
perfume, dust and linen, dark
wood and sunlight through the
skylight, across the room.

Paralucent Condensed Light 10pt

PAINTING MYSELF WAVING
GOODBYE, gilt-framed and hung
high, linseed oil and canvas
perfume, dust and linen, dark
wood and sunlight through the
skylight, across the room.

Paralucent Condensed Medium 10pt

PAINTING MYSELF WAVING
GOODBYE, gilt-framed and hung
high, linseed oil and canvas
perfume, dust and linen, dark
wood and sunlight through the
skylight, across the room.

Paralucent Condensed Extra Light Italic 10pt

PAINTING MYSELF WAVING
GOODBYE, gilt-framed and hung
high, linseed oil and canvas
perfume, dust and linen, dark
wood and sunlight through the
skylight, across the room.

Paralucent Condensed Light Italic 10pt

PAINTING MYSELF WAVING
GOODBYE, gilt-framed and hung
high, linseed oil and canvas
perfume, dust and linen, dark
wood and sunlight through the
skylight, across the room.

Paralucent Condensed Medium Italic 10pt

PLEASE NOTE
an optional service charge of
10% will be added to your bill.
Thank you for your cooperation.

Paralucent Condensed Bold 62pt and Medium Italic 35pt

PAINTING MYSELF WAVING
GOODBYE, gilt-framed and hung
high, linseed oil and canvas
perfume, dust and linen, dark
wood and sunlight through the
skylight, across the room.

Paralucent Condensed Demi Bold 10pt

PAINTING MYSELF WAVING
GOODBYE, gilt-framed and hung
high, linseed oil and canvas
perfume, dust and linen, dark
wood and sunlight through the
skylight, across the room.

Paralucent Condensed Bold 10pt

PAINTING MYSELF WAVING
GOODBYE, gilt-framed and hung
high, linseed oil and canvas
perfume, dust and linen, dark
wood and sunlight through the
skylight, across the room.

Paralucent Condensed Heavy 10pt

PAINTING MYSELF WAVING
GOODBYE, gilt-framed and hung
high, linseed oil and canvas
perfume, dust and linen, dark
wood and sunlight through the
skylight, across the room.

Paralucent Condensed Demi Bold Italic 10pt

PAINTING MYSELF WAVING
GOODBYE, gilt-framed and hung
high, linseed oil and canvas
perfume, dust and linen, dark
wood and sunlight through the
skylight, across the room.

Paralucent Condensed Bold Italic 10pt

PAINTING MYSELF WAVING
GOODBYE, gilt-framed and hung
high, linseed oil and canvas
perfume, dust and linen, dark
wood and sunlight through the
skylight, across the room.

Paralucent Condensed Heavy Italic 10pt

DNA

Quagmire Black 200pt

THE TRANSFER OF DESIRED CHARACTERISTICS between unrelated species, or even between plants and animals, enhances body customisation possibilities.

Quagmire Medium 10pt

THE TRANSFER OF DESIRED CHARACTERISTICS between unrelated species, or even between plants and animals, enhances body customisation possibilities.

Quagmire Medium Italic 10pt

THE TRANSFER OF DESIRED CHARACTERISTICS between unrelated species, or even between plants and animals, enhances body customisation possibilities.

Quagmire Demi 10pt

THE TRANSFER OF DESIRED CHARACTERISTICS between unrelated species, or even between plants and animals, enhances body customisation possibilities.

Quagmire Demi Italic 10pt

THE TRANSFER OF DESIRED CHARACTERISTICS between unrelated species, or even between plants and animals, enhances body customisation possibilities.

Quagmire Bold 10pt

THE TRANSFER OF DESIRED CHARACTERISTICS between unrelated species, or even between plants and animals, enhances body customisation possibilities.

Quagmire Bold Italic 10pt

THE TRANSFER OF DESIRED CHARACTERISTICS between unrelated species, or even between plants and animals, enhances body customisation possibilities.

Quagmire Black 10pt

THE TRANSFER OF DESIRED CHARACTERISTICS between unrelated species, or even between plants and animals, enhances body customisation possibilities.

Quagmire Black Italic 10pt

THE TRANSFER OF CHARACTERISTICS between unrelated species enhances body customisation possibilities.

Quagmire Medium Extended 10pt

THE TRANSFER OF CHARACTERISTICS between unrelated species enhances body customisation possibilities.

Quagmire Medium Extended Italic 10pt

THE TRANSFER OF CHARACTERISTICS between unrelated species enhances body customisation possibilities.

Quagmire Bold Extended 10pt

THE TRANSFER OF CHARACTERISTICS between unrelated species enhances body customisation possibilities.

Quagmire Bold Extended Italic 10pt

Scientific

Quagmire Medium Extended 70pt

Manipulation of the basic building blocks of life itself

Quagmire Bold Extended 25pt

Test bed

Quagmire Black 93pt

DRUM BEAT

Range Light 10pt

The tang of burning metal;
nearside headlight blindness;
ten-lane arterial ringroad east

Range Light 10pt

Sample Rate

Range Light 10pt

A SYMPHONY BUILT FROM FOUND SOUNDS: the looped protesting
squeal of worn rubber on wet tarmac, the weighty churning of
gargantuan machinery in an automobile assembly plant, and the
bleeps, clicks and ticks of a mainframe computer hub.

Range Light 10pt

A SYMPHONY BUILT FROM FOUND SOUNDS: the looped protesting
squeal of worn rubber on wet tarmac, the weighty churning of
gargantuan machinery in an automobile assembly plant, and the
bleeps, clicks and ticks of a mainframe computer hub.

Range Medium 10pt

A SYMPHONY BUILT FROM FOUND SOUNDS: the looped protesting
squeal of worn rubber on wet tarmac, the weighty churning of
gargantuan machinery in an automobile assembly plant, and the
bleeps, clicks and ticks of a mainframe computer hub.

Range Bold 10pt

A SYMPHONY BUILT FROM FOUND SOUNDS: the looped protesting
squeal of worn rubber on wet tarmac, the weighty churning of
gargantuan machinery in an automobile assembly plant, and the
bleeps, clicks and ticks of a mainframe computer hub.

Range Extra Bold 10pt

A SYMPHONY BUILT FROM FOUND SOUNDS: the looped protesting
squeal of worn rubber on wet tarmac, the weighty churning of
gargantuan machinery in an automobile assembly plant, and the
bleeps, clicks and ticks of a mainframe computer hub.

Range Black 10pt

Fast, Wide, Narrow

Range Medium 34pt

UNITS 1-7

Regulator Cameo 60pt

Alternate versions of &, capital R and K, and the lower case g and r are available as follows: [Alt m]: &; [Alt ,]: g; [Alt .]: g̃; [Alt =]: r, [Alt 5]: R; [Shift-Alt §]: K.

Regulator Light 11pt

Communications

Regulator Bold 47pt

VOGUE

Regulator Heavy 110pt

Consultations, scientific research, consumer information, industry groups, information, licensing and numbering.

Regulator Thin 13pt

Consultations, scientific research, consumer information, industry groups, information, licensing and numbering.

Regulator Light 13pt

Consultations, scientific research, consumer information, industry groups, information, licensing and numbering.

Regulator Medium 13pt

Consultations, scientific research, consumer information, industry groups, information, licensing and numbering.

Regulator Bold 13pt

Consultations, scientific research, consumer information, industry groups, information, licensing and numbering.

Regulator Heavy 13pt

MISSION STATEMENT

Regulator Light 75pt

Outreach programs

Regulator Bold 42pt

Television and radio telecommunications

Regulator Medium 40pt

breaker

Regulator Thin Italic 107pt

High bandwidth furthers the interests of citizen-consumers as the communications industries enter the age of direct transmission delivery.

Regulator Thin 8pt

High bandwidth furthers the interests of citizen-consumers as the communications industries enter the age of direct transmission delivery.

Regulator Thin Italic 8pt

High bandwidth furthers the interests of citizen-consumers as the communications industries enter the age of direct transmission delivery.

Regulator Light 8pt

High bandwidth furthers the interests of citizen-consumers as the communications industries enter the age of direct transmission delivery.

Regulator Light Italic 8pt

High bandwidth furthers the interests of citizen-consumers as the communications industries enter the age of direct transmission delivery.

Regulator Medium 8pt

High bandwidth furthers the interests of citizen-consumers as the communications industries enter the age of direct transmission delivery.

Regulator Medium Italic 8pt

High bandwidth furthers the interests of citizen-consumers as the communications industries enter the age of direct transmission delivery.

Regulator Bold 8pt

High bandwidth furthers the interests of citizen-consumers as the communications industries enter the age of direct transmission delivery.

Regulator Bold Italic 8pt

High bandwidth furthers the interests of citizen-consumers as the communications industries enter the age of direct transmission delivery.

Regulator Heavy 8pt

High bandwidth furthers the interests of citizen-consumers as the communications industries enter the age of direct transmission delivery.

Regulator Heavy Italic 8pt

End-user licencing

Regulator Light 47pt

CONSULTATIONS, SCIENTIFIC RESEARCH, CONSUMER INFORMATION, INDUSTRY GROUPS, INFORMATION, LICENSING AND NUMBERING.

Regulator Thin 12pt

CONSULTATIONS, SCIENTIFIC RESEARCH, CONSUMER INFORMATION, INDUSTRY GROUPS, INFORMATION, LICENSING AND NUMBERING.

Regulator Light 12pt

CONSULTATIONS, SCIENTIFIC RESEARCH, CONSUMER INFORMATION, INDUSTRY GROUPS, INFORMATION, LICENSING AND NUMBERING.

Regulator Medium 12pt

CONSULTATIONS, SCIENTIFIC RESEARCH, CONSUMER INFORMATION, INDUSTRY GROUPS, INFORMATION, LICENSING AND NUMBERING.

Regulator Bold 12pt

CONSULTATIONS, SCIENTIFIC RESEARCH, CONSUMER INFORMATION, INDUSTRY GROUPS, INFORMATION, LICENSING AND NUMBERING.

Regulator Heavy 12pt

Lounge bar

Darkside Regular 204pt

Commonwealth festival

Ainsdale Medium and Ainsdale Bold 63pt

SHINY

Bingo 96pt

COMPUTER LOVE

Contour Regular and Contour Outline 30pt

SLAPDOWN

Doom Platoon Medium and Doom Platoon Bold 56pt

Brooklyn Heights Mission

Gargoyle 47pt

Poppycock

Blackcurrant Alternates 50pt

Intercom NewsPlus

Gravel Bold, Gravel Medium and Gravel Medium Italic 43pt

Acacia Grange

Wexford Oakley 54pt

Fandango GTR

Gran Turismo Extended 33ptt

whizz

Griffin Italic 120ptt

BOXTER

Hounslow Shadow 90pt

Floral Aromas

Novak Spring and Novak Winter 45pt

Terminal City recycling plant

Platinum and Platinum Inline 20pt

KNOB TWIDDLER
keyboard king

Register Light 45pt and Register Bold 50pt

GREAT

Scrotnig 83pt

GRUNGER

Untitled 1 70pt

DF Acton

One
One Italic
Two
Two Italic

The quick brown Fox jumps over the lazy dog.
THE QUICK BROWN FOX JUMPS OVER THE LAZY DOG.

The quick brown Fox jumps over the lazy dog.
THE QUICK BROWN FOX JUMPS OVER THE LAZY DOG.

The quick brown Fox jumps over the lazy dog.
THE QUICK BROWN FOX JUMPS OVER THE LAZY DO

ABCDEFGHIJKLMNOPQRSTUVWXYZ
abcdefghijklmnopqrstuvwxyz
1234567890 ,.;:?!%oE$¢&#{[]}@©

ABCDEFGHIJKLMNOPQRSTUVWXYZ
abcdefghijklmnopqrstuvwxyz
1234567890 ,.;:?!%oE$¢&#{[]}@©

ABCDEFGHIJKLMNOPQRSTUVWXYZ
abcdefghijklmnopqrstuvwxyz
1234567890 ,.;:?!%oE$¢&#{[]}@©

ABCDEFGHIJKLMNOPQRSTUVWXYZ
abcdefghijklmnopqrstuvwxyz
1234567890 ,.;:?!%oE$¢&#{[]}@©

DF Ainsdale

Medium
Medium Italic
Bold
Bold Italic

The quick brown Fox jumps over the lazy dog.
THE QUICK BROWN FOX JUMPS OVER THE LAZY DOG.
The quick brown Fox jumps over the lazy dog.
THE QUICK BROWN FOX JUMPS OVER THE LAZY DOG.
The quick brown Fox jumps over the lazy dog.
THE QUICK BROWN FOX JUMPS OVER THE LAZY DOG.

ABCDEFGHIJKLMNOPQRSTUVWXYZ 1234567890
abcdefghijklmnopqrstuvwxyz ,.;:?!%oE$¢&#{[]}@©

ABCDEFGHIJKLMNOPQRSTUVWXYZ 1234567890
abcdefghijklmnopqrstuvwxyz ,.;:?!%oE$¢&#{[]}@©

ABCDEFGHIJKLMNOPQRSTUVWXYZ 1234567890
abcdefghijklmnopqrstuvwxyz |·|.·?!%o£$¢&#{[]}@©

ABCDEFGHIJKLMNOPQRSTUVWXYZ 1234567890
abcdefghijklmnopqrstuvwxyz |·|.·?!%o£$¢&#{[]}@©

DF Amorpheus

Regular
Alternates

THE QUICK BROWN FOX JUMPS OVER THE LAZY DOG.
THE QUICK BROWN FOX JUMPS OVER THE LAZY DOG.

THE QUICK BROWN FOX JUMPS OVER THE LAZY DOG.
THE QUICK BROWN FOX JUMPS OVER THE LAZY DOG.

THE QUICK BROWN FOX JUMPS OVER THE L
THE QUICK BROWN FOX JUMPS OVER THE L

G ±, G alt.

ABCDEFGHIJKLMNOPQRSTUVWXYZ
ABCDEFGHIJKLMNOPQRSTUVWXYZ
1234567890 ,.,::?!%o£$¢&№(())AT©

ABCDEFGHIJKLMNOPQRSTUVWXYZ
ABCDEFGHIJKLMNOPQRSTUVWXYZ
1234567890 ,.,::?!%o£$¢&№(())AT©

TRANCER!

Amorpheous Alternates 74pt

DF Anytime Now

Regular

Create custom clock faces featuring any time you desire (in 5 minute increments).

DF Autofont

Regular

DF Bingo

Regular

tHe QuICK BROWN FOX JUMPS OVeR tHe LaZy DOG.
tHe QuICK BROWN FOX JUMPS OVeR tHe LaZy DOG.

tHe QuICK BROWN FOX JUMPS OVeR tHe LaZy
tHe QuICK BROWN FOX JUMPS OVeR tHe LaZy

tHe QuICK BROWN FOX JUMPS OVeR
tHe QuICK BROWN FOX JUMPS OVeR

ABCDEFGHIJKLMNOPQRSTUVWXYZ
ABCDEFGHIJKLMNOPQRSTUVWXYZ
1234567890 ,.;:?!%£$¢&#(())@©

DF Blackcurrant

Black
Squash
Cameo

THE QUICK BROWN FOX JUMPS OVER THE LAZY DO
THE QUICK BROWN FOX JUMPS OVER THE LAZY DO

THE QUICK BROWN FOX JUMPS OVE
THE QUICK BROWN FOX JUMPS OVE

THE QUICK BROWN FOX JUM
THE QUICK BROWN FOX JUM

ABCDEFGHIJKLMNOPQRSTUVWXYZ
ABCDEFGHIJKLMNOPQRSTUVWXYZ
1234567890 ,.;:?!%£$‡&№:(())@©

ABCDEFGHIJKLMNOPQRSTUVWXYZ
ABCDEFGHIJKLMNOPQRSTUVWXYZ
1234567890 ,.;:?!%£$‡&№:(())@©

ABCDEFGHIJKLMNOPQRSTUVWXYZ
ABCDEFGHIJKLMNOPQRSTUVWXYZ
1234567890 ,.;:?!%£$‡&№:(())@©

DF Blackcurrant Alternates

Black Alternates
Sqaush Alternates

The quick brown fox jumps over the lazy dog.
THE QUICK BROWN FOX JUMPS OVER THE LAZY DOG.

The quick brown fox jumps over the
THE QUICK BROWN FOX JUMPS

The quick brown fox jumps
THE QUICK BROWN FOX

ABCDEFGHIJKLMNOPQRSTUVWXYZ
abcdefghijklmnopqrstuvwxyz
1234567890 ,.;:?!%£$¢&ℕº‹()›@©

ABCDEFGHIJKLMNOPQRSTUVWXYZ
abcdefghijklmnopqrstuvwxyz
1234567890 ,.;:?!%£$¢&ℕº‹()›@©

Blackcurrant Squash 83pt

DF Bordello

Bold
Bold Italic
Shaded

❋ alt ., ✿ alt ., ✱ alt m, ✼ alt d, ✷ alt w, ☎ alt l, ◉ alt v, ✪ alt j.

THE QUICK BROWN FOX JUMPS OVER THE LAZY DOG.
The quick brown fox jumps over the lazy dog.
THE QUICK BROWN FOX JUMPS OVER THE LAZY
The quick brown fox jumps over the 1
THE QUICK BROWN FOX JUMPS OV

ABCDEFGHIJKLMNOPQRSTUVWXYZ
abcdefghijklmnopqrstuvwxyz
1234567890 ,.;:?!%£$¢&#(()))@©

ABCDEFGHIJKLMNOPQRSTUVWXYZ
abcdefghijklmnopqrstuvwxyz
1234567890 ,.;:?!%£$¢&#(()))@©

ABCDEFGHIJKLMNOPQRSTUVWXYZ
abcdefghijklmnopqrstuvwxyz
1234567890 ,.;:?!%£$¢&#(()))@©

DF Bullroller

Regular

the quick brown fox jumps over the lazy dog.
THE QUICK BROWN FOX JUMPS OVER THE LAZY DOG.

the quick brown fox jumps over the lazy dog.
THE QUICK BROWN FOX JUMPS OVER THE LAZY DOG.

the quick brown fox jumps over the
THE QUICK BROWN FOX JUMPS OVER THE

ABCDEFGHIJKLMNOPQRSTUVWXYZ
abcdefghijklmnopqrstuvwxyz
1234567890 .,:;?!%£$¢&#[()]@©

DF Cantaloupe

Regular

The quick brown fox jumps over the lazy dog.
THE QUICK BROWN FOX JUMPS OVER THE LAZY DOG.

The quick brown fox jumps over the lazy
THE QUICK BROWN FOX JUMPS OVER THE

The quick brown fox jumps ove
THE QUICK BROWN FOX JUMPS

ABCDEFGHIJKLMNOPQRSTUVWXYZ
abcdefghijklmnopqrstuvwxyz
1234567890 .,:;?!%£$¢&#[()]@©

DF Chascarillo

Regular

The quick brown fox jumps over the lazy dog.   8 alt., R alt., + alt 5, + ±.
THE QUICK BROWN FOX JUMPS OVER THE LAZY DOG.

The quick brown fox jumps over the lazy dog.
THE QUICK BROWN FOX JUMPS OVER THE LA

The quick brown fox jumps over the lazy dog.
THE QUICK BROWN FOX JUMPS OVER

ABCDEFGHIJKLMNOPQRSTUVWXYZ
abcdefghijklmnopqrstuvwxyz
1234567890 .,:;?!%£$$&#{()}@©

DF Citrus

Regular

The quick brown fox jumps over the lazy dog
THE QUICK BROWN FOX JUMPS OVER THE LAZY DOG

The quick brown fox jumps over the
THE QUICK BROWN FOX JUMPS OV

The quick brown fox jump
THE QUICK BROWN FOX J

ABCDEFGHIJKLMNOPQRSTUVWXYZ
abcdefghijklmnopqrstuvwxyz
1234567890 .,:;?!%£$¢$#[()]@©

DF Contour

Regular
Italic
Outline
Shaded

→ alt 5, ← ±, ¨ alt „, ʊ alt m, ✳ alt d, ☎ alt w, ♥ alt b, ⊁ alt 9, ⫪ alt 0, ✚ alt z.

THE QUICK BROWN FOX JUMPS OVER THE LAZY
THE QUICK BROWN FOX JUMPS OVER THE LAZY

THE QUICK BROWN FOX JUMPS OVE
THE QUICK BROWN FOX JUMPS OVE

THE QUICK BROWN FOX JUM
THE QUICK BROWN FOX JUM

ABCDEFGHIJKLMNOPQRS
TUVWXYZ 1234567890
ƪ¡ʅ¿?!%‰£€$¢&#()ⒶⓉⒸ

*ABCDEFGHIJKLMNOPQRS
TUVWXYZ 1234567890
ƪ¡ʅ¿?!%‰£€$¢&#()ⒶⓉⒸ*

ABCDEFGHIJKLMNOPQRS
TUVWXYZ 1234567890
ƪ¡ʅ¿?!%‰£€$¢&#()ⒶⓉⒸ

ABCDEFGHIJKLMNOPQRS
TUVWXYZ 1234567890
ƪ¡ʅ¿?!%‰£€$¢&#()ⒶⓉⒸ

DF Cordite

Regular
Inline

THE QUICK BROWN FOX JUMPS OVER THE LAZY DOG
THE QUICK BROWN FOX JUMPS OVER THE LAZY DOG

THE QUICK BROWN FOX JUMPS OVER T
THE QUICK BROWN FOX JUMPS OVER T

THE QUICK BROWN FOX JUMPS
THE QUICK BROWN FOX JUMPS

ABCDEFGHIJKLMNOPQRSTU
VWXYZ 1234567890
ƪ¡ʅ¿?!%/£$¢&✳()ⒶⒹⒸ

ABCDEFGHIJKLMNOPQRSTU
VWXYZ 1234567890
ƪ¡ʅ¿?!%/£$¢&✳()ⒶⒹⒸ

DF Cottingley

Regular
Word Beginnings
Word Ends

the quick brown fox jumps over the lazy dog.
the quick brown fox jumps over the lazy dog.

the quick brown fox jumps over the lazy dog.
the quick brown fox jumps over the lazy dog.

the quick brown fox jumps over the
the quick brown fox jumps over the

abcdefghijklmnopqrstuvwxyz
abcdefghijklmnopqrstuvwxyz
1234567890 .,:;?!%±£$¢&no () at

Three fonts make up Cottingley, a linking script. These three fonts
are manually combined as shown in the example below. The "capitals"
provide extensions to the bar of the lower case "t".
End flourishes are available at: alt v, alt x, alt l.

clementine

l/c Word Beginnings   l/c Regular   l/c Regular   l/c Regular   l/c Regular   l/c Regular   u/c Regular   u/c Regular   u/c Regular   l/c Word Ends

DF Cyberdelic!

Regular

THE QUICK BROWN FOX JUMPS OVER THE LAZY DOG.
THE QUICK BROWN FOX JUMPS OVER THE LAZY DOG.

THE QUICK BROWN FOX JUMPS OVER THE LAZY DOG.
THE QUICK BROWN FOX JUMPS OVER THE LAZY DOG.

THE QUICK BROWN FOX JUMPS OVER TH
THE QUICK BROWN FOX JUMPS OVER TH

ABCDEFGHIJKLMNOPQRSTUVWXYZ
ABCDEFGHIJKLMNOPQRSTUVWXYZ
1234567890 ..:;?!%£$¢&$(()]@©

DF Darkside

Regular
Italic
Bright

alt 5. alt ., alt m, alt d, alt w, shift alt p, alt p, alt b, alt ,, alt ±, alt z.
the quick brown fox jumps over the lazy dog.
the quick brown fox jumps over the lazy dog.
the quick brown fox jumps over the lazy dog.

abcdefghijklmnopqrstuvwxyz ,.:;?!%£$¢&#{[()]}@©
1234567890

abcdefghijklmnopqrstuvwxyz ,.:;?!%£$¢&#{[()]}@©
1234567890

abcdefghijklmnopqrstuvwxyz .,:;?!%¬abcdefghij*{[()]}@©
1234567890

DF Data 90

Regular
Outline
Shaded

THE QUICK BROWN FOX JUMPS OVER THE LAZY DOG.
THE QUICK BROWN FOX JUMPS OVER THE LAZY DOG.

THE QUICK BROWN FOX JUMPS OVER THE
THE QUICK BROWN FOX JUMPS OVER THE

THE QUICK BROWN FOX JUMPS
THE QUICK BROWN FOX JUMPS

ABCDEFGHIJKLMNOPQRSTUVWXYZ
ABCDEFGHIJKLMNOPQRSTUVWXYZ
1234567890 ,.:;?!%£$¢&#{()}@©

ABCDEFGHIJKLMNOPQRSTUVWXYZ
ABCDEFGHIJKLMNOPQRSTUVWXYZ
1234567890 ,.:;?!%£$¢&#{()}@©

ABCDEFGHIJKLMNOPQRSTUVWXYZ
ABCDEFGHIJKLMNOPQRSTUVWXYZ
1234567890 ,.:;?!%£$¢&#{()}@©

**DF Doom
Platoon**

Medium
Bold

THE QUICK BROWN FOX JUMPS OVER THE LAZY DOG.
THE QUICK BROWN FOX JUMPS OVER THE LAZY DOG.

THE QUICK BROWN FOX JUMPS OVER THE L
THE QUICK BROWN FOX JUMPS OVER THE L

THE QUICK BROWN FOX JUMPS
THE QUICK BROWN FOX JUMPS

ABCDEFGHIJKLMNOPQRSTUVWXYZ
1234567890
,.:;?!%£$¢&#{()}

ABCDEFGHIJKLMNOPQRSTUVWXYZ
1234567890
,.:;?!%£$¢&#{()}

DF Elektron

Light
Medium
Bold
Shaded

The quick brown fox jumps over the lazy dog.
THE QUICK BROWN FOX JUMPS OVER THE LAZY DOG.

The quick brown fox jumps over the lazy dog.
THE QUICK BROWN FOX JUMPS OVER THE LA

The quick brown fox jumps over the
THE QUICK BROWN FOX JUMPS OU

ABCDEFGHIJKLMNOPQRSTUVWXYZ
abcdefghijklmnopqrstuvwxyz
1234567890 ,.:;?!%ʃ£$¢&#[[]]@©

ABCDEFGHIJKLMNOPQRSTUVWXYZ
abcdefghijklmnopqrstuvwxyz
1234567890 ,.:;?!%ʃ£$¢&#[[]]@©

ABCDEFGHIJKLMNOPQRSTUVWXYZ
abcdefghijklmnopqrstuvwxyz
1234567890 ,.:;?!%ʃ£$¢&#[[]]@©

ABCDEFGHIJKLMNOPQRSTUVWXYZ
abcdefghijklmnopqrstuvwxyz
1234567890 ,.:;?!%ʃ£$¢&#[[]]@©

DF English Grotesque

Thin
Light
Medium
Bold
Extra Bold
Black

The quick brown fox jumps over the lazy   J alt j, ǫ alt 5, & alt m, £ alt v.
THE QUICK BROWN FOX JUMPS OVER THE LAZY DOG.

The quick brown fox jumps over the lazy dog.
THE QUICK BROWN FOX JUMPS OVER THE LAZY D

The quick brown fox jumps over the lazy
THE QUICK BROWN FOX JUMPS OVER

ABCDEFGHIJKLMNOPQRSTUVWXYZ
abcdefghijklmnopqrstuvwxyz
1234567890 ,.:;?!%£$¢&⁄Nº{()}@©

ABCDEFGHIJKLMNOPQRSTUVWXYZ
abcdefghijklmnopqrstuvwxyz
1234567890 ,.:;?!%£$¢&⁄Nº{()}@©

ABCDEFGHIJKLMNOPQRSTUVWXYZ
abcdefghijklmnopqrstuvwxyz
1234567890 ,.;:?!%£$¢&№{()}@©

ABCDEFGHIJKLMNOPQRSTUVWXYZ
abcdefghijklmnopqrstuvwxyz
1234567890 ,.;:?!%£$¢&№{()}@©

ABCDEFGHIJKLMNOPQRSTUVWXYZ
abcdefghijklmnopqrstuvwxyz
1234567890 ,.;:?!%£$¢&№{()}@©

ABCDEFGHIJKLMNOPQRSTUVWXYZ
abcdefghijklmnopqrstuvwxyz
1234567890 ,.;:?!%£$¢&№{()}@©

DF Flak

Regular
Nailed
Spraycard

The quick brown fox jumps over the lazy dog.
THE QUICK BROWN FOX JUMPS OVER THE LAZY DOG.

The quick brown fox jumps over the lazy dog.
THE QUICK BROWN FOX JUMPS OVER THE LAZY DOG.

The quick brown fox jumps over the lazy dog.
THE QUICK BROWN FOX JUMPS OVER THE LAZY DOG.

ABCDEFGHIJKLMNOPQRSTUVWXYZ abcdefghijklmno
pqrstuvwxyz 1234567890 ,.;:?!%£$¢&#[()]@©

ABCDEFGHIJKLMNOPQRSTUVWXYZ abcdefghijklmno
pqrstuvwxyz 1234567890 ,.;:?!%£$¢&#[()]@©

ABCDEFGHIJKLMNOPQRSTUVWXYZ
abcdefghijklmnopqrstuvwxyz
1234567890 ,.;:?!%&#[()]@©£$¢

DF Flak Heavy

Heavy

The quick brown fox jumps over the lazy dog.
THE QUICK BROWN FOX JUMPS OVER THE LAZY DOG.

The quick brown fox jumps over the lazy do
THE QUICK BROWN FOX JUMPS OVER THE

The quick brown fox jumps over the
THE QUICK BROWN FOX JUMPS OV

ABCDEFGHIJKLMNOPQRSTUVWXYZ
abcdefghijklmnopqrstuvwxyz
1234567890 ,.;:?!%£$¢&-/+[[.]]@@©

DF Foonky

Heavy
Starred

The quick brown fox jumps over the lazy dog.
THE QUICK BROWN FOX JUMPS OVER THE LAZY DOG.

The quick brown fox jumps over the lazy dog
THE QUICK BROWN FOX JUMPS OVER THE LAZY

The quick brown fox jumps over th
THE QUICK BROWN FOX JUMPS OVER

ABCDEFGHIJKLMNOPQRSTUVWXYZ
abcdefghijklmnopqrstuvwxyz
1234567890 ,.;:?!%£$¢&n?(()}@©

ABCDEFGHIJKLMNOPQRSTUVWXYZ
abcdefghijklmnopqrstuvwxyz
1234567890 ,.;:?!%£$¢&n?(()}@©

DF Freeman

Regular
Italic
Black
Black Italic

The quick brown fox jumps over the lazy dog.
THE QUICK BROWN FOX JUMPS OVER THE LAZY DOG.

The quick brown fox jumps over the lazy dog.
THE QUICK BROWN FOX JUMPS OVER THE LAZY DOG.

The quick brown fox jumps over the lazy dog.
THE QUICK BROWN FOX JUMPS OVER THE LAZY DOG.

g alt ,.

ABCDEFGHIJKLMNOPQRSTUVWXYZ 1234567890
abcdefghijklmnopqrstuvwxyz ,.,:?!%£$¡&#

ABCDEFGHIJKLMNOPQRSTUVWXYZ 1234567890
abcdefghijklmnopqrstuvwxyz ,.,:?!%£$¡&#

ABCDEFGHIJKLMNOPQRSTUVWXYZ 1234567890
abcdefghijklmnopqrstuvwxyz ,.;:?!%£§¿&#

ABCDEFGHIJKLMNOPQRSTUVWXYZ 1234567890
abcdefghijklmnopqrstuvwxyz ,.;:?!%£§¿&#

DF Game Over

Shaded

THE QUICK BROWN FOX JUMPS OVER THE LAZY DOG.
THE QUICK BROWN FOX JUMPS OVER THE LAZY DOG.

THE QUICK BROWN FOX JUMPS OVER THE LAZY DOG.
THE QUICK BROWN FOX JUMPS OVER THE LAZY DOG.

THE QUICK BROWN FOX JUMPS OVER T
THE QUICK BROWN FOX JUMPS OVER T

ABCDEFGHIJKLMNOPQRSTUVWXYZ
1234567890
.,!?!%£$¢&#(())@©

DF Gargoyle

Black
Cameo

The quick brown fox jumps over the lazy dog.
THE QUICK BROWN FOX JUMPS OVER THE LAZY DOG.

The quick brown fox jumps over the lazy dog.
THE QUICK BROWN FOX JUMPS OVER THE LAZY DOG.

The quick brown fox jumps over the lazy dog.
THE QUICK BROWN FOX JUMPS OVER THE LAZY DOG.

ABCDEFGHIJKLMNOPQRSTUVWXYZ 1234567890
abcdefghijklmnopqrstuvwxyz ,.;:?!%£§¿&№°

Oblique Magnifique

Gargoyle Cameo
and Black 64pt

DF Gran Turismo

Regular
Italic
Outline
Shaded

The quick brown fox jumps over the lazy dog.
THE QUICK BROWN FOX JUMPS OVER THE LAZY DOG.

The quick brown fox jumps over the lazy dog.
THE QUICK BROWN FOX JUMPS OVER THE

The quick brown fox jumps over the lazy
THE QUICK BROWN FOX JUMPS OVER

ABCDEFGHIJKLMNOPQRSTUVWXYZ
abcdefghijklmnopqrstuvwxyz
1234567890 ...::?!%.$$¢£¥?{<>}

ABCDEFGHIJKLMNOPQRSTUVWXYZ
abcdefghijklmnopqrstuvwxyz
1234567890 ...::?!%.$$¢£¥?{<>}

ABCDEFGHIJKLMNOPQRSTUVWXYZ
abcdefghijklmnopqrstuvwxyz
1234567890 ...::?!%.$$¢£¥?{<>}

ABCDEFGHIJKLMNOPQRSTUVWXYZ
abcdefghijklmnopqrstuvwxyz
1234567890 ...::?!%.$$¢£¥?{<>}

DF Gran Turismo Extended

Extended
Extended Italic

The quick brown fox jumps over the lazy dog.
THE QUICK BROWN FOX JUMPS OVER THE LAZY

The quick brown fox jumps over the
THE QUICK BROWN FOX JUMPS OV

The quick brown fox jumps o
THE QUICK BROWN FOX JU

ABCDEFGHIJKLMNOPQRSTUVWXYZ
abcdefghijklmnopqrstuvwxyz
1234567890 ...::?!%.$$¢£¥?{<>}

ABCDEFGHIJKLMNOPQRSTUVWXYZ
abcdefghijklmnopqrstuvwxyz
1234567890 ...::?!%.$$¢£¥?{<>}

DF Gravel

Light
Light Italic
Medium
Medium Italic
Bold
Bold Italic

The quick brown fox jumps over the lazy dog.
THE QUICK BROWN FOX JUMPS OVER THE LAZY DOG.
The quick brown fox jumps over the lazy dog.
THE QUICK BROWN FOX JUMPS OVER THE LAZY DOG.
The quick brown fox jumps over the lazy dog.
THE QUICK BROWN FOX JUMPS OVER THE LAZY DOG.

ABCDEFGHIJKLMNOPQRSTUVWXYZ
abcdefghijklmnopqrstuvwxyz
1234567890 ,.;:?!%£$¢&#{([])}@©

ABCDEFGHIJKLMNOPQRSTUVWXYZ
abcdefghijklmnopqrstuvwxyz
1234567890 ,.;:?!%£$¢&#{([])}@©

ABCDEFGHIJKLMNOPQRSTUVWXYZ
abcdefghijklmnopqrstuvwxyz
1234567890 ,.;:?!%£$¢&#{([])}@©

ABCDEFGHIJKLMNOPQRSTUVWXYZ
abcdefghijklmnopqrstuvwxyz
1234567890 ,.;:?!%£$¢&#{([])}@©

ABCDEFGHIJKLMNOPQRSTUVWXYZ
abcdefghijklmnopqrstuvwxyz
1234567890 ,.;:?!%£$¢&#{([])}@©

ABCDEFGHIJKLMNOPQRSTUVWXYZ
abcdefghijklmnopqrstuvwxyz
1234567890 ,.;:?!%£$¢&#{([])}@©

Corporate i.d.

Gravel Medium and Bold 67pt   Features kerned ligatures

DF Griffin

Black
Italic
Shaded
Dynamo Capitals

The quick brown fox jumps
THE QUICK BROWN FOX JUMPS OVER THE LAZY DOG.

X alt m, **A** alt d, **A** alt w, **M** shift alt p.

The quick brown fox jumps over the lazy dog,
THE QUICK BROWN FOX JUMPS OVER THE LAZY DO

The quick brown fox jumps o
THE QUICK BROWN FOX JUMPS

ABCDEFGHIJKLMNOPQRSTUVWXYZ
abcdefghijklmnopqrstuvwxyz
1234567890 ,.;:"?!%£$¢&№[()]@®

ABCDEFGHIJKLMNOPQRSTUVWXYZ
abcdefghijklmnopqrstuvwxyz
1234567890 ,.;:"?!%£$¢&№[()]@®

ABCDEFGHIJKLMNOPQRSTUVWXYZ
abcdefghijklmnopqrstuvwxyz
1234567890 ,.;:"?!%£$¢&№[()]@®

ABCDEFGHIJKLMNOPQRSTUVWXYZ
abcdefghijklmnopqrstuvwxyz
1234567890 ,.;:"?!%£$¢&№[()]@®

**DF Haulage
Commercial**

Bold
Bold Italic
Striped
Striped Italic

THE QUICK BROWN FOX JUMPS OVER THE LAZY DOG.
THE QUICK BROWN FOX JUMPS OVER THE LAZY DOG.

THE QUICK BROWN FOX JUMPS OVER THE LAZY DOG.
THE QUICK BROWN FOX JUMPS OVER THE LAZY DOG.

THE QUICK BROWN FOX JUMPS OVER THE
THE QUICK BROWN FOX JUMPS OVER THE

AABBCCDDEEFFGGHHII JJKKLLMMNNOOPP
QQRRSSTTUUVVWWXXYYZZ 1234567890
,.;:?!%£$¢&#[()]@© Not intended for caps-only use

AABBCCDDEEFFGGHHII JJKKLLMMNNOOPP
QQRRSSTTUUVVWWXXYYZZ 1234567890
,.;:?!%£$¢&#[()]@© Not intended for caps-only use

AABBCCDDEEFFGGHHIIJJKKLLMMNNOOPP
QQRRSSTTUUUUUUWWXXYYZZ 1234567890
.,:;?!%₀₀E$¢&#{()}@© Not intended for caps-only use

AABBCCDDEEFFGGHHIIJJKKLLMMNNOOPP
QQRRSSTTUUUUUUWWXXYYZZ 1234567890
.,:;?!%₀₀E$¢&#{()}@© Not intended for caps-only use

Haulage
Commercial
Striped Italic
and Bold Italic 78pt

DF Hounslow

Open
Shadow
Solid
Open Italic
Shadow Italic
Solid Italic

THE QUICK BROWN FOX JUMPS OVER THE LAZY DOG.
THE QUICK BROWN FOX JUMPS OVER THE LAZY DOG.
THE QUICK BROWN FOX JUMPS OVER THE LAZY DOG.
THE QUICK BROWN FOX JUMPS OVER THE LAZY DOG.
THE QUICK BROWN FOX JUMPS OVER
THE QUICK BROWN FOX JUMPS OVER

ABCDEFGHIJKLMNOPQRSTUVWXYZ
ABCDEFGHIJKLMNOPQRSTUVWXYZ
1234567890 .,:;?!%₀₀E$¢&#{()}

ABCDEFGHIJKLMNOPQRSTUVWXYZ
ABCDEFGHIJKLMNOPQRSTUVWXYZ
1234567890 .,:;?!%₀₀E$¢&#{()}

ABCDEFGHIJKLMNOPQRSTUVWXYZ
ABCDEFGHIJKLMNOPQRSTUVWXYZ
1234567890 .,:;?!%₀₀E$¢&#{()}

ABCDEFGHIJKLMNOPQRSTUVWXYZ
ABCDEFGHIJKLMNOPQRSTUVWXYZ
1234567890 .,:;?!%₀₀E$¢&#{()}

ABCDEFGHIJKLMNOPQRSTUVWXYZ
ABCDEFGHIJKLMNOPQRSTUVWXYZ
1234567890 ,.;:?!%bE$¢&#{[]}

ABCDEFGHIJKLMNOPQRSTUVWXYZ
ABCDEFGHIJKLMNOPQRSTUVWXYZ
1234567890 ,.;:?!%bE$¢&#{[]}

DF Iconics

One
Two
Three
Four

Iconics Four 75pt

DF Jakita

Wide
Wide Inline
Wide Bold

The quick brown Fox jumps over the lazy dog.
THE QUICK BROWN FOX JUMPS OVER THE LAZY

The quick brown Fox jumps ov
THE QUICK BROWN FOX JUMPS

The quick brown Fox ju
THE QUICK BROWN FOX

RBCDEFGHIJKLMNOPQRSTUVWXYZ
abcdeFghijklmnopqrstuvwxyz
1234567890 ,.::?!%oE$¢&#+()}-回回

RBCDEFGHIJKLMNOPQRSTUVWXYZ
abcdeFghijklmnopqrstuvwxyz
1234567890 ,.::?!%oE$¢&#+()}-回回

RBCDEFGHIJKLMNOPQRSTUVWXYZ
abcdeFghijklmnopqrstuvwxyz
1234567890 ,.::?!%oE$¢&#+()}-回回

DF Jemima

Regular
Italic
Shadow

THE QUICK BROWN FOX JUMPS OVER THE LAZY DOG.
THE QUICK BROWN FOX JUMPS OVER THE LAZY DOG.

THE QUICK BROWN FOX JUMPS OVER THE LAZY DOG.
THE QUICK BROWN FOX JUMPS OVER THE LAZY DOG.

THE QUICK BROWN FOX JUMPS OVER THE L
THE QUICK BROWN FOX JUMPS OVER THE L

ABCDEFGHIJKLMNOPQRSTUVWXYZ
ABCDEFGHIJKLMNOPQRSTUVWXYZ
1234567890 ,.:;:?!%£$¢&#-(())-

ABCDEFGHIJKLMNOPQRSTUVWXYZ
ABCDEFGHIJKLMNOPQRSTUVWXYZ
1234567890 ,.:;:?!%£$¢&#-(())-

ABCDEFGHIJKLMNOPQRSTUVWXYZ
ABCDEFGHIJKLMNOPQRSTUVWXYZ
1234567890 ,.:;:?!%£$¢&#-(())-Ⓐ©

DF Judgement A

Medium
Medium Italic
Bold
Bold Italic
Black
Black Italic

THE QUICK BROWN FOX JUMPS OVER THE LAZY DOG.
THE QUICK BROWN FOX JUMPS OVER THE LAZY DOG.

THE QUICK BROWN FOX JUMPS OVER THE LAZY DOG.
THE QUICK BROWN FOX JUMPS OVER THE LAZY DOG.

THE QUICK BROWN FOX JUMPS OVER THE LAZY DO
THE QUICK BROWN FOX JUMPS OVER THE LAZY DO

ABCDEFGHIJKLMNOPQRSTUVWXYZ
ABCDEFGHIJKLMNOPQRSTUVWXYZ
1234567890 ,.;:?!%o£$¢&№{[]}@©

ABCDEFGHIJKLMNOPQRSTUVWXYZ
ABCDEFGHIJKLMNOPQRSTUVWXYZ
1234567890 ,.;:?!%o£$¢&№{[]}@©

ABCDEFGHIJKLMNOPQRSTUVWXYZ
ABCDEFGHIJKLMNOPQRSTUVWXYZ
1234567890 ,.;:?!%o£$¢&№{[]}@©

ABCDEFGHIJKLMNOPQRSTUVWXYZ
ABCDEFGHIJKLMNOPQRSTUVWXYZ
1234567890 ,.;:?!%o£$¢&№{[]}@©

ABCDEFGHIJKLMNOPQRSTUVWXYZ
ABCDEFGHIJKLMNOPQRSTUVWXYZ
1234567890 ,.;:?!%o£$¢&№{[]}@©

ABCDEFGHIJKLMNOPQRSTUVWXYZ
ABCDEFGHIJKLMNOPQRSTUVWXYZ
1234567890 ,.;:?!%o£$¢&№{[]}@©

LOCKDOWN

Judgement Black and Judgement Black Italic 60pt

DF Judgement B

Compressed
Compressed Italic
Compressed Inline
Black Condensed
Black Cond. Italic
Icons

THE QUICK BROWN FOX JUMPS OVER THE LAZY DOG.
THE QUICK BROWN FOX JUMPS OVER THE LAZY DOG.

THE QUICK BROWN FOX JUMPS OVER THE LAZY DOG.
THE QUICK BROWN FOX JUMPS OVER THE LAZY DOG.

THE QUICK BROWN FOX JUMPS OVER THE LAZY DOG.
THE QUICK BROWN FOX JUMPS OVER THE LAZY DOG.

ABCDEFGHIJKLMNOPQRSTUVWXYZ ABCDEFGHIJKLMN
OPQRSTUVWXYZ 1234567890 ,.;:?!℧o£$¢&№[[]]@©

ABCDEFGHIJKLMNOPQRSTUVWXYZ ABCDEFGHIJKLMN
OPQRSTUVWXYZ 1234567890 ,.;:?!℧o£$¢&№[[]]@©

ABCDEFGHIJKLMNOPQRSTUVWXYZ ABCDEFGHIJKLMN
OPQRSTUVWXYZ 1234567890 ,.;:?!℧o£$¢&№[[]]@©

JUDGE AND JURY

Judgement Black Condensed, Judgement Compressed Inline and Judgement Black Condensed Italic 64pt

ABCDEFGHIJKLMNOPQRSTUVWXYZ
ABCDEFGHIJKLMNOPQRSTUVWXYZ
1234567890 ,.;:?!℧o£$¢&№[[]]@©

ABCDEFGHIJKLMNOPQRSTUVWXYZ
ABCDEFGHIJKLMNOPQRSTUVWXYZ
1234567890 ,.;:?!℧o£$¢&№[[]]@©

REALITY CHECK! · THE END · ★★ · U13 · NEW THRILL · HE'S BACK! · FREE! · THEY'RE BACK! · ★ · SHE'S BACK! · STARTS TODAY! · FREE GIFT! · WIN! · NEXT PROG · ! · ? · ← · ↓ · → · ↺ · ↙ · ↱ · ↖ · PART 1 · PART 2 · PART 3 · PART 4 · PART 5 · PART 6 · PART 7 · PART 8 · PART 9 · PART 10 · PART 11 · PART 12 · PART 13 · PART 14 · PART 15 · PART 16 · PART 17 · PART 18 · PART 19 · PART 20 · PART 21 · PART 22 · PART 23 · PART 24 · PART 25 · PART 26 · ◀◀ · ▶▶ · ▲ · ▼ · ▶ · ◀ · ▼ · ■ · □

DF Judgement C

Black Embossed
Black Highlight
Black Rimmed
Black Shadow
Black Stencil
Black Stencil Italic

THE QUICK BROWN FOX JUMPS OVER THE LAZY DOG.
THE QUICK BROWN FOX JUMPS OVER THE LAZY DOG.

THE QUICK BROWN FOX JUMPS OVER THE LAZY DOG.
THE QUICK BROWN FOX JUMPS OVER THE LAZY DOG.

THE QUICK BROWN FOX JUMPS OVER
THE QUICK BROWN FOX JUMPS OVER

ABCDEFGHIJKLMNOPQRSTUVWXYZ
ABCDEFGHIJKLMNOPQRSTUVWXYZ
1234567890 ,.;:?!%₀£$¢&№(|)@©

ABCDEFGHIJKLMNOPQRSTUVWXYZ
ABCDEFGHIJKLMNOPQRSTUVWXYZ
1234567890 ,.;:?!%₀£$¢&№(|)@©

ABCDEFGHIJKLMNOPQRSTUVWXYZ
ABCDEFGHIJKLMNOPQRSTUVWXYZ
1234567890 ,.;:?!%₀£$¢&№(|)@©

ABCDEFGHIJKLMNOPQRSTUVWXYZ
ABCDEFGHIJKLMNOPQRSTUVWXYZ
1234567890 ,.;:?!%₀£$¢&№(|)@©

ABCDEFGHIJKLMNOPQRSTUVWXYZ
ABCDEFGHIJKLMNOPQRSTUVWXYZ
1234567890 ,.;:?!%₀£$¢&№(|)@©

ABCDEFGHIJKLMNOPQRSTUVWXYZ
ABCDEFGHIJKLMNOPQRSTUVWXYZ
1234567890 ,.;:?!%₀£$¢&№(|)@©

Judgement Black Embossed and Judgement Black Stencil 64pt

DF Klaxon

One
One Outline
Two
Two Outline

THE QUICK BROWN FOX JUMPS OVER THE LAZY DOG.
THE QUICK BROWN FOX JUMPS OVER THE LAZY DOG.

THE QUICK BROWN FOX JUMPS OVER THE LAZY DOG.
THE QUICK BROWN FOX JUMPS OVER THE LAZY DOG.

THE QUICK BROWN FOX JUMPS OVER THE LA
THE QUICK BROWN FOX JUMPS OVER THE LA

ABCDEFGHIJKLMNOPQRSTUVWXYZ
ABCDEFGHIJKLMNOPQRSTUVWXYZ
1234567890 ,.;:?!/.£$¢&✳((::))∂Ø

ABCDEFGHIJKLMNOPQRSTUVWXYZ
ABCDEFGHIJKLMNOPQRSTUVWXYZ
1234567890 ,.;:?!/.£$¢&✳((::))∂Ø

ABCDEFGHIJKLMNOPQRSTUVWXYZ
ABCDEFGHIJKLMNOPQRSTUVWXYZ
1234567890 ,.;:?!/.£$¢&✳((::))∂Ø

ABCDEFGHIJKLMNOPQRSTUVWXYZ
ABCDEFGHIJKLMNOPQRSTUVWXYZ
1234567890 ,.;:?!/.£$¢&✳((::))∂Ø

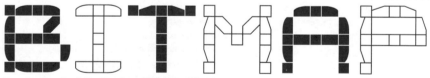

Klaxon One, Klaxon One Outline, Klaxon Two and Klaxon Two Outline 76pt

DF Laydeez Nite

Regular

THE QUICK BROWN FOX JUMPS OVER THE LAZY DOG.
THE QUICK BROWN FOX JUMPS OVER THE LAZY DOG.

THE QUICK BROWN FOX JUMPS OVER THE LAZY DOG.
THE QUICK BROWN FOX JUMPS OVER THE LAZY DOG.

THE QUICK BROWN FOX JUMPS OVER THE LAZY DO
THE QUICK BROWN FOX JUMPS OVER THE LAZY DO

abcdefghijklmnopqrstuvwxyz
1234567890 ,.;:#?!0/$=$¢&#(())@Ø

DF Lusta A

Forty Sans
Eighty Sans
Forty Serif
Eighty Serif

The quick brown fox jumps over the lazy dog.
THE QUICK BROWN FOX JUMPS OVER THE LAZY DOG.
The quick brown fox jumps over the lazy dog.
THE QUICK BROWN FOX JUMPS OVER THE LAZY DOG.
The quick brown fox jumps over the lazy dog.
THE QUICK BROWN FOX JUMPS OVER THE LAZY DOG.

ABCDEFGHIJKLMNOPQRSTUVWXYZ abcdefghijklmno
pqrstuvwxyz 1234567890 .,.;!?!'7.£$¢€№?(()}@©

ABCDEFGHIJKLMNOPQRSTUVWXYZ abcdefghijklmno
pqrstuvwxyz 1234567890 .,.;!?!'7.£$¢€№?(()}@©

ABCDEFGHIJKLMNOPQRSTUVWXYZ abcdefghijklmno
pqrstuvwxyz 1234567890 .,.;!?!'7.£$¢€№?(()}@©

ABCDEFGHIJKLMNOPQRSTUVWXYZ abcdefghijklmno
pqrstuvwxyz 1234567890 .,.;!?!'7.£$¢€№?(()}@©

DF Lusta B

One Twenty Sans
One Sixty Sans
Two Hundred Sans

The quick brown fox jumps over the lazy dog.
THE QUICK BROWN FOX JUMPS OVER THE LAZY DOG.
The quick brown fox jumps over the lazy dog.
THE QUICK BROWN FOX JUMPS OVER THE LAZY DOG.
The quick brown fox jumps over the lazy dog.
THE QUICK BROWN FOX JUMPS OVER THE LAZY DOG.

ABCDEFGHIJKLMNOPQRSTUVWXYZ abcdefghijklmno
pqrstuvwxyz 1234567890 .,.;!?!'7.£$¢€№?(()}@©

ABCDEFGHIJKLMNOPQRSTUVWXYZ abcdefghijklmno
pqrstuvwxyz 1234567890 .,.;!?!'7.£$¢€№?(()}@©

ABCDEFGHIJKLMNOPQRSTUVWXYZ abcdefghijklmno pqrstuvwxyz 1234567890 ,.:!?!?.£$¢&°{}@©

Lusta One Sixty Sans and
Lusta One Twenty Sans 94pt

DF Mac Dings

Regular

DF Mastertext

Light
Plain
Heavy
Boxed
Symbols One
Symbols Two

THE QUICK BROWN FOX JUMPS OVER THE LAZY DOG.
THE QUICK BROWN FOX JUMPS OVER THE LAZY DOG.
THE QUICK BROWN FOX JUMPS OVER THE LAZY DOG.
THE QUICK BROWN FOX JUMPS OVER THE LAZY DOG.
THE QUICK BROWN FOX JUMPS OVER THE LAZY
THE QUICK BROWN FOX JUMPS OVER THE LAZY

← alt p, ↑ shift alt p,
→ alt w, ↓ alt b, ◇ alt j.

ABCDEFGHIJKLMNOPQRSTUVWXYZ
ABCDEFGHIJKLMNOPQRSTUVWXYZ
1234567890 ,.:;?!%£$¢&#(()) ⊐©

ABCDEFGHIJKLMNOPQRSTUVWXYZ
ABCDEFGHIJKLMNOPQRSTUVWXYZ
1234567890 ,.:;?!%£$¢&#(()) ⊐©

ABCDEFGHIJKLMNOPQRSTUVWXYZ
ABCDEFGHIJKLMNOPQRSTUVWXYZ
1234567890 ,.:;?!%£$¢&#(()) ⊐©

DF MenSwear

Regular

DF Mercano Empire

Regular
Italic

The quick brown fox jumps over the lazy dog.
THE QUICK BROWN FOX JUMPS OVER THE LAZY DOG.

The quick brown fox jumps over the lazy dog.
THE QUICK BROWN FOX JUMPS OVER THE LAZY DOG.

The quick brown fox jumps over the lazy dog.
THE QUICK BROWN FOX JUMPS OVER THE LAZY DOG.

ABCDEFGHIJKLMNOPQRSTUVWXYZ 1234567890
abcdefghijklmnopqrstuvwxyz ,.;:?!%o£$¢&#@©

ABCDEFGHIJKLMNOPQRSTUVWXYZ 1234567890
abcdefghijklmnopqrstuvwxyz ,.;:?!%o£$¢&#@©

DF Mercano Empire Condensed

Regular
Italic

The quick brown fox jumps over the lazy dog.
THE QUICK BROWN FOX JUMPS OVER THE LAZY DOG.

The quick brown fox jumps over the lazy dog.
THE QUICK BROWN FOX JUMPS OVER THE LAZY DOG.

The quick brown fox jumps over the lazy dog.
THE QUICK BROWN FOX JUMPS OVER THE LAZY DOG.

ABCDEFGHIJKLMNOPQRSTUVWXYZ 1234567890
abcdefghijklmnopqrstuvwxyz ,.;:?!%œ£§¢&#@©{[]}

ABCDEFGHIJKLMNOPQRSTUVWXYZ 1234567890
abcdefghijklmnopqrstuvwxyz ,.;:?!%œ£§¢&#@©{[]}

DF Mercano Empire Lined

Regular
Italic

The quick brown fox jumps over the lazy dog.
THE QUICK BROWN FOX JUMPS OVER THE LAZY DOG.

The quick brown fox jumps over the lazy dog.
THE QUICK BROWN FOX JUMPS OVER THE LAZY DOG.

The quick brown fox jumps over the lazy dog.
THE QUICK BROWN FOX JUMPS OVER THE LAZY DOG.

ABCDEFGHIJKLMNOPQRSTUVWXYZ 1234567890
abcdefghijklmnopqrstuvwxyz ,.;:?!%œ£§¢&#@©{[]}

ABCDEFGHIJKLMNOPQRSTUVWXYZ 1234567890
abcdefghijklmnopqrstuvwxyz ,.;:?!%œ£§¢&#@©{[]}

DF Metropol Noir

Regular

THE QUICK BROWN FOX JUMPS OVER THE LAZY DOG.
THE QUICK BROWN FOX JUMPS OVER THE LAZY DOG.

THE QUICK BROWN FOX JUMPS OVER THE LAZY D
THE QUICK BROWN FOX JUMPS OVER THE LAZY DO

THE QUICK BROWN FOX JUMPS OVER TH
THE QUICK BROWN FOX JUMPS OVER THE

ABCDEFGHIJKLMNOPQRSTUVWXYZ
ABCDEFGHIJKLMNOPQRSTUVWXYZ
1234567890 ,.;:?!%£$¢&№[()]@©

DF Motorcity

Regular

DF Mystique

Blacque
Fantasie
Cosmique

THE QUICK BROWN FOX JUMPS OVER THE LAZY DOG.
THE QUICK BROWN FOX JUMPS OVER THE LAZY DOG.

THE QUICK BROWN FOX JUMPS OVER THE LA
THE QUICK BROWN FOX JUMPS OVER THE LA

THE QUICK BROWN FOX JUMPS
THE QUICK BROWN FOX JUMPS

ABCDEFGHIJKLMNOPQRSTUVWXYZ
ABCDEFGHIJKLMNOPQRSTUVWXYZ
1234567890 ..::??!%£¢‡‖&*[()]◐◭◉

ABCDEFGHIJKLMNOPQRSTUVWXYZ
ABCDEFGHIJKLMNOPQRSTUVWXYZ
1234567890 ..::??!%£¢‡‖&*[()]◐◭◉

ABCDEFGHIJKLMNOPQRSTUVWXYZ
ABCDEFGHIJKLMNOPQRSTUVWXYZ
1234567890 ..::??!%£¢‡‖&*[()]◐◭◉

DF Novak

Winter
Spring

The quick brown fox jumps over the lazy dog.
THE QUICK BROWN FOX JUMPS OVER THE LAZY DOG.
The quick brown fox jumps over the lazy dog.
THE QUICK BROWN FOX JUMPS OVER THE LAZY DOG

The quick brown fox jumps over the
THE QUICK BROWN FOX JUMPS O

⚘ alt w.

ABCDEFGHIJKLMNOPQRSTUVWXYZ
abcdefghijklmnopqrstuvwxyz
1234567890 ,.:;??!%£$¢&#[()]ⓐⓒ

ABCDEFGHIJKLMNOPQRSTUVWXYZ
abcdefghijklmnopqrstuvwxyz
1234567890 ,.;:?!%£\$¢&#[()]@©

DF Paralucent A

Extra Light
Extra Light Italic
Medium
Medium Italic
Bold
Bold Italic

The quick brown fox jumps over the lazy dog.
THE QUICK BROWN FOX JUMPS OVER THE LAZY DOG.

f ±, t alt „ R alt m.

The quick brown fox jumps over the lazy dog.
THE QUICK BROWN FOX JUMPS OVER THE LAZY DOG.

The quick brown fox jumps over the lazy dog.
THE QUICK BROWN FOX JUMPS OVER THE LAZY

ABCDEFGHIJKLMNOPQRSTUVWXYZ
abcdefghijklmnopqrstuvwxyz
1234567890 ,.;:?!%£\$¢&#[()]@©

ABCDEFGHIJKLMNOPQRSTUVWXYZ
abcdefghijklmnopqrstuvwxyz
1234567890 ,.;:?!%£\$¢&#[()]@©

ABCDEFGHIJKLMNOPQRSTUVWXYZ
abcdefghijklmnopqrstuvwxyz
1234567890 ,.;:?!%£\$¢&#[()]@©

ABCDEFGHIJKLMNOPQRSTUVWXYZ
abcdefghijklmnopqrstuvwxyz
1234567890 ,.;:?!%£\$¢&#[()]@©

ABCDEFGHIJKLMNOPQRSTUVWXYZ
abcdefghijklmnopqrstuvwxyz
1234567890 ,.;:?!%£\$¢&#[()]@©

ABCDEFGHIJKLMNOPQRSTUVWXYZ
abcdefghijklmnopqrstuvwxyz
1234567890 ,.;:?!%£\$¢&#[()]@©

DF Paralucent B

Thin
Thin Italic
Light
Light Italic
Demi Bold
Demi Bold Italic
Heavy
Heavy Italic

The quick brown fox jumps over the lazy dog
THE QUICK BROWN FOX JUMPS OVER THE LAZY DOG.

The quick brown fox jumps over the lazy dog.
THE QUICK BROWN FOX JUMPS OVER THE LAZY DOG.

The quick brown fox jumps over the lazy dog.
THE QUICK BROWN FOX JUMPS OVER THE LAZY

f ±, t alt „ R alt m.

ABCDEFGHIJKLMNOPQRSTUVWXYZ
abcdefghijklmnopqrstuvwxyz
1234567890 ,.;:?!%o£$¢&#[()]@©

ABCDEFGHIJKLMNOPQRSTUVWXYZ
abcdefghijklmnopqrstuvwxyz
1234567890 ,.;:?!%o£$¢&#[()]@©

ABCDEFGHIJKLMNOPQRSTUVWXYZ
abcdefghijklmnopqrstuvwxyz
1234567890 ,.;:?!%o£$¢&#[()]@©

ABCDEFGHIJKLMNOPQRSTUVWXYZ
abcdefghijklmnopqrstuvwxyz
1234567890 ,.;:?!%o£$¢&#[()]@©

ABCDEFGHIJKLMNOPQRSTUVWXYZ
abcdefghijklmnopqrstuvwxyz
1234567890 ,.;:?!%o£$¢&#[()]@©

ABCDEFGHIJKLMNOPQRSTUVWXYZ
abcdefghijklmnopqrstuvwxyz
1234567890 ,.;:?!%o£$¢&#[()]@©

ABCDEFGHIJKLMNOPQRSTUVWXYZ
abcdefghijklmnopqrstuvwxyz
1234567890 ,.;:?!%o£$¢&#[()]@©

ABCDEFGHIJKLMNOPQRSTUVWXYZ
abcdefghijklmnopqrstuvwxyz
1234567890 ,.;:?!%£$¢&#[()]@©

**DF Paralucent
Condensed A**

Extra Light
Extra Light Italic
Medium
Medium Italic
Bold
Bold Italic

Ea1

The quick brown fox jumps over the lazy dog.
THE QUICK BROWN FOX JUMPS OVER THE LAZY DOG.

The quick brown fox jumps over the lazy dog.
THE QUICK BROWN FOX JUMPS OVER THE LAZY DOG.

The quick brown fox jumps over the lazy dog.
THE QUICK BROWN FOX JUMPS OVER THE LAZY DOG.

f±, t alt „ R alt m.

ABCDEFGHIJKLMNOPQRSTUVWXYZ
abcdefghijklmnopqrstuvwxyz
1234567890 ,.;:?!%£$¢&#[()]@©

ABCDEFGHIJKLMNOPQRSTUVWXYZ
abcdefghijklmnopqrstuvwxyz
1234567890 ,.;:?!%£$¢&#[()]@©

ABCDEFGHIJKLMNOPQRSTUVWXYZ
abcdefghijklmnopqrstuvwxyz
1234567890 ,.;:?!%£$¢&#[()]@©

ABCDEFGHIJKLMNOPQRSTUVWXYZ
abcdefghijklmnopqrstuvwxyz
1234567890 ,.;:?!%£$¢&#[()]@©

ABCDEFGHIJKLMNOPQRSTUVWXYZ
abcdefghijklmnopqrstuvwxyz
1234567890 ,.;:?!%£$¢&#[()]@©

ABCDEFGHIJKLMNOPQRSTUVWXYZ
abcdefghijklmnopqrstuvwxyz
1234567890 ,.;:?!%£$¢&#[()]@©

DF Paralucent Condensed B
Thin
Thin Italic
Light
Light Italic
Demi
Demi Italic
Heavy
Heavy Italic

Ea1

The quick brown fox jumps over the lazy dog.
THE QUICK BROWN FOX JUMPS OVER THE LAZY DOG.

The quick brown fox jumps over the lazy dog.
THE QUICK BROWN FOX JUMPS OVER THE LAZY DOG.

The quick brown fox jumps over the lazy dog.
THE QUICK BROWN FOX JUMPS OVER THE LAZY DOG.

f ±, t alt „ R alt m.

ABCDEFGHIJKLMNOPQRSTUVWXYZ
abcdefghijklmnopqrstuvwxyz
1234567890 „.,:?!%o£$¢&#[()]@©

ABCDEFGHIJKLMNOPQRSTUVWXYZ
abcdefghijklmnopqrstuvwxyz
1234567890 „.,:?!%o£$¢&#[()]@©

ABCDEFGHIJKLMNOPQRSTUVWXYZ
abcdefghijklmnopqrstuvwxyz
1234567890 „.,:?!%o£$¢&#[()]@©

ABCDEFGHIJKLMNOPQRSTUVWXYZ
abcdefghijklmnopqrstuvwxyz
1234567890 „.,:?!%o£$¢&#[()]@©

ABCDEFGHIJKLMNOPQRSTUVWXYZ
abcdefghijklmnopqrstuvwxyz
1234567890 „.,:?!%o£$¢&#[()]@©

ABCDEFGHIJKLMNOPQRSTUVWXYZ
abcdefghijklmnopqrstuvwxyz
1234567890 „.,:?!%o£$¢&#[()]@©

ABCDEFGHIJKLMNOPQRSTUVWXYZ
abcdefghijklmnopqrstuvwxyz
1234567890 „.,:?!%o£$¢&#[()]@©

ABCDEFGHIJKLMNOPQRSTUVWXYZ
abcdefghijklmnopqrstuvwxyz
1234567890 ,.;:?!%o£$¢&#[()]@©

**DF Paralucent
Stencil**

Extra Light
Medium
Bold

The quick brown fox jumps over the lazy dog.
THE QUICK BROWN FOX JUMPS OVER THE LAZY DOG.

f±, t alt „ R alt m.

The quick brown fox jumps over the lazy dog.
THE QUICK BROWN FOX JUMPS OVER THE LAZY DOG.

The quick brown fox jumps over the lazy dog.
THE QUICK BROWN FOX JUMPS OVER THE LAZY

ABCDEFGHIJKLMNOPQRSTUVWXYZ
abcdefghijklmnopqrstuvwxyz
1234567890 ,.;:?!%o£$¢&#[()]@©

ABCDEFGHIJKLMNOPQRSTUVWXYZ
abcdefghijklmnopqrstuvwxyz
1234567890 ,.;:?!%o£$¢&#[()]@©

ABCDEFGHIJKLMNOPQRSTUVWXYZ
abcdefghijklmnopqrstuvwxyz
1234567890 ,.;:?!%o£$¢&#[()]@©

DF Pic Format

Regular

Pic
Format
Regular 78pt

DF Platinum

Regular
Inline

The quick brown fox jumps over the lazy dog. *W* alt ., *M* alt m, **E** ±.
THE QUICK BROWN FOX JUMPS OVER THE LAZY DOG.

The quick brown fox jumps over the lazy dog.
THE QUICK BROWN FOX JUMPS OVER THE LAZY D

The quick brown fox jumps over the
THE QUICK BROWN FOX JUMPS OVER

ABCDEFGHIJKLMNOPQRSTUVWXYZ
abcdefghijklmnopqrstuvwxyz
1234567890 ..,:?!%£$¢&#{()}@©

ABCDEFGHIJKLMNOPQRSTUVWXYZ
abcdefghijklmnopqrstuvwxyz
1234567890 ..:?!%£$¢&#{()}@©

DF Popgod

Regular

The quick brown fox jumps over the lazy dog.
THE QUICK BROWN FOX JUMPS OVER THE LAZY DOG.

The quick brown fox jumps over the lazy dog.
THE QUICK BROWN FOX JUMPS OVER THE LAZY D

The quick brown fox jumps over the lazy
THE QUICK BROWN FOX JUMPS OVER THE

ABCDEFGHIJKLMNOPQRSTUVWXYZ
abcdefghijklmnopqrstuvwxyz
1234567890 ,.;:?!%£$¢&#{()}@©

Popgod Regular 92pt

DF Quagmire A

Medium
Medium Italic
Bold
Bold Italic

The quick brown fox jumps over the lazy dog.   **B** alt m.
THE QUICK BROWN FOX JUMPS OVER THE LAZY DOG.

The quick brown fox jumps over the lazy dog.
THE QUICK BROWN FOX JUMPS OVER THE LAZY DOG.

The quick brown fox jumps over the lazy do
THE QUICK BROWN FOX JUMPS OVER THE LA

ABCDEFGHIJKLMNOPQRSTUVWXYZ
abcdefghijklmnopqrstuvwxyz
1234567890 ,.;:?!%£$3o&#[()]@©

ABCDEFGHIJKLMNOPQRSTUVWXYZ
abcdefghijklmnopqrstuvwxyz
1234567890 ,.;:?!%o£$¢&#[()]@©

ABCDEFGHIJKLMNOPQRSTUVWXYZ
abcdefghijklmnopqrstuvwxyz
1234567890 ,.;:?!%o£$¢&#[()]@©

ABCDEFGHIJKLMNOPQRSTUVWXYZ
abcdefghijklmnopqrstuvwxyz
1234567890 ,.;:?!%o£$¢&#[()]@©

DF Quagmire B

Demi
Demi Italic
Black
Black Italic

The quick brown fox jumps over the lazy dog.   B alt m.
THE QUICK BROWN FOX JUMPS OVER THE LAZY DOG.
The quick brown fox jumps over the lazy dog.
THE QUICK BROWN FOX JUMPS OVER THE LAZY DOG.
The quick brown fox jumps over the lazy
THE QUICK BROWN FOX JUMPS OVER THE

ABCDEFGHIJKLMNOPQRSTUVWXYZ
abcdefghijklmnopqrstuvwxyz
1234567890 ,.;:?!%o£$¢&#[()]@©

ABCDEFGHIJKLMNOPQRSTUVWXYZ
abcdefghijklmnopqrstuvwxyz
1234567890 ,.;:?!%o£$¢&#[()]@©

ABCDEFGHIJKLMNOPQRSTUVWXYZ
abcdefghijklmnopqrstuvwxyz
1234567890 ,.;:?!%o£$¢&#[()]@©

ABCDEFGHIJKLMNOPQRSTUVWXYZ
abcdefghijklmnopqrstuvwxyz
1234567890 ,.;:?!%o£$¢&#[()]@©

DF Quagmire Extended

Medium
Medium Italic
Bold
Bold Italic

Ea1

B alt m.

The quick brown fox jumps over the lazy dog.
THE QUICK BROWN FOX JUMPS OVER THE LAZY DOG.

The quick brown fox jumps over the lazy do
THE QUICK BROWN FOX JUMPS OVER THE LA

The quick brown fox jumps over the la
THE QUICK BROWN FOX JUMPS OVER T

ABCDEFGHIJKLMNOPQRSTUVWXYZ
abcdefghijklmnopqrstuvwxyz
1234567890 ,.:;?!%o£$¢&#[()}@©

ABCDEFGHIJKLMNOPQRSTUVWXYZ
abcdefghijklmnopqrstuvwxyz
1234567890 ,.:;?!%o£$¢&#[()}@©

ABCDEFGHIJKLMNOPQRSTUVWXYZ
abcdefghijklmnopqrstuvwxyz
1234567890 ,.:;?!%o£$¢&#[()}@©

ABCDEFGHIJKLMNOPQRSTUVWXYZ
abcdefghijklmnopqrstuvwxyz
_1234567890 ,.:;?!%o£$¢&#[()}@©_

DF Range

Light
Medium
Bold
Extra Bold
Black

Ea1

K alt w.

The quick brown fox jumps over the lazy dog.
THE QUICK BROWN FOX JUMPS OVER THE LAZY DOG.

The quick brown fox jumps over the lazy dog.
THE QUICK BROWN FOX JUMPS OVER THE LAZY DOG.

The quick brown fox jumps over the
THE QUICK BROWN FOX JUMPS OVER TH

ABCDEFGHIJKLMNOPQRSTUVWXYZ
abcdefghijklmnopqrstuvwxyz
1234567890 ,.:;?!%£$¢&#[()}@©

ABCDEFGHIJKLMNOPQRSTUVWXYZ
abcdefghijklmnopqrstuvwxyz
1234567890 ,.:;?!%£$¢&#[()}@©

ABCDEFGHIJKLMNOPQRSTUVWXYZ
abcdefghijklmnopqrstuvwxyz
1234567890 ,.;:?!%£$¢&#[()]@©

ABCDEFGHIJKLMNOPQRSTUVWXYZ
abcdefghijklmnopqrstuvwxyz
1234567890 ,.;:?!%£$¢&#[()]@©

ABCDEFGHIJKLMNOPQRSTUVWXYZ
abcdefghijklmnopqrstuvwxyz
1234567890 ,.;:?!%£$¢&#[()]@©

SputnikUSA

Range Light and Range Black 61pt

DF Reasonist

Medium
Medium Italic

☺ alt 5, ☻ ±, ✖ alt ., ♥ alt ., ☎ alt m,
☺ alt d, ☻ alt w, ☻ shift alt p, ☻ shift alt 7.

THE QUICK BROWN FOX JUMPS OVER THE LAZY DOG.
THE QUICK BROWN FOX JUMPS OVER THE LA
THE QUICK BROWN FOX JUMPS OVER
THE QUICK BROWN FOX JUMPS

ABCDEFGHIJKLMNOPQRSTUVWXYZ
ABCDEFGHIJKLMNOPQRSTUVWXYZ
1234567890 .,:;?!%£$¢&ℕº{()}ᴬᵀ©

ABCDEFGHIJKLMNOPQRSTUVWXYZ
ABCDEFGHIJKLMNOPQRSTUVWXYZ
1234567890 .,:;?!%£$¢&ℕº{()}ᴬᵀ©

Reasonist Medium Italic 81pt

CHERRY!

DF Register A

Light
Light Italic
Demi Bold
Demi Bold Italic

The quick brown fox jumps over the lazy dog.
THE QUICK BROWN FOX JUMPS OVER THE LAZY DOG.
The quick brown fox jumps over the lazy dog.
THE QUICK BROWN FOX JUMPS OVER THE LAZ
The quick brown fox jumps over the
THE QUICK BROWN FOX JUMPS OVER

ABCDEFGHIJKLMNOPQRSTUVWXYZ
abcdefghijklmnopqrstuvwxyz
1234567890 .,:;?!%£$¢&#{[]}@©

ABCDEFGHIJKLMNOPQRSTUVWXYZ
abcdefghijklmnopqrstuvwxyz
1234567890 .,:;?!%£$¢&#{[]}@©

ABCDEFGHIJKLMNOPQRSTUVWXYZ
abcdefghijklmnopqrstuvwxyz
1234567890 .,:;?!%£$¢&#{[]}@©

ABCDEFGHIJKLMNOPQRSTUVWXYZ
abcdefghijklmnopqrstuvwxyz
1234567890 .,:;?!%£$¢&#{[]}@©

DF Register B

Extra Light
Extra Light Italic
Medium
Medium Italic
Bold
Bold Italic

The quick brown fox jumps over the lazy dog.
THE QUICK BROWN FOX JUMPS OVER THE LAZY DOG.
The quick brown fox jumps over the lazy dog.
THE QUICK BROWN FOX JUMPS OVER THE LAZ
The quick brown fox jumps over the
THE QUICK BROWN FOX JUMPS OVER

ABCDEFGHIJKLMNOPQRSTUVWXYZ
abcdefghijklmnopqrstuvwxyz
1234567890 .,:;?!%£$¢&#{[]}@©

ABCDEFGHIJKLMNOPQRSTUVWXYZ
abcdefghijklmnopqrstuvwxyz
1234567890 .,:;?!%£$¢&#{[]}@©

ABCDEFGHIJKLMNOPQRSTUVWXYZ
abcdefghijklmnopqrstuvwxyz
1234567890 ,.:;?!%£$¢&#{[()]}@©

ABCDEFGHIJKLMNOPQRSTUVWXYZ
abcdefghijklmnopqrstuvwxyz
1234567890 ,.:;?!%£$¢&#{[()]}@©

ABCDEFGHIJKLMNOPQRSTUVWXYZ
abcdefghijklmnopqrstuvwxyz
1234567890 ,.:;?!%£$¢&#{[()]}@©

ABCDEFGHIJKLMNOPQRSTUVWXYZ
abcdefghijklmnopqrstuvwxyz
1234567890 ,.:;?!%£$¢&#{[()]}@©

**DF Register
Wide A**

Light
Light Italic
Demi Bold
Demi Bold Italic

The quick brown fox jumps over the lazy dog.
THE QUICK BROWN FOX JUMPS OVER THE LAZY DOG.

The quick brown fox jumps over the lazy do
THE QUICK BROWN FOX JUMPS OVER THE LA

The quick brown fox jumps ove
THE QUICK BROWN FOX JUMPS

ABCDEFGHIJKLMNOPQRSTUVWXYZ
abcdefghijklmnopqrstuvwxyz
1234567890 ,.:;?!%£$¢&#{[()]}@©

ABCDEFGHIJKLMNOPQRSTUVWXYZ
abcdefghijklmnopqrstuvwxyz
1234567890 ,.:;?!%£$¢&#{[()]}@©

ABCDEFGHIJKLMNOPQRSTUVWXYZ
abcdefghijklmnopqrstuvwxyz
1234567890 ,.:;?!%£$¢&#{[()]}@©

ABCDEFGHIJKLMNOPQRSTUVWXYZ
abcdefghijklmnopqrstuvwxyz
1234567890 ..:;?!%₀£$¢&#{[]}@©

**DF Register
Wide B**

Extra Light
Extra Light Italic
Medium
Medium Italic
Bold
Bold Italic

The quick brown fox jumps over the lazy dog.
THE QUICK BROWN FOX JUMPS OVER THE LAZY DOG.

The quick brown fox jumps over the lazy do
THE QUICK BROWN FOX JUMPS OVER THE LA

The quick brown fox jumps ove
THE QUICK BROWN FOX JUMPS

ABCDEFGHIJKLMNOPQRSTUVWXYZ
abcdefghijklmnopqrstuvwxyz
1234567890 ..:;?!%₀£$¢&#{[]}@©

ABCDEFGHIJKLMNOPQRSTUVWXYZ
abcdefghijklmnopqrstuvwxyz
1234567890 ..:;?!%₀£$¢&#{[]}@©

ABCDEFGHIJKLMNOPQRSTUVWXYZ
abcdefghijklmnopqrstuvwxyz
1234567890 ..:;?!%₀£$¢&#{[]}@©

ABCDEFGHIJKLMNOPQRSTUVWXYZ
abcdefghijklmnopqrstuvwxyz
1234567890 ..:;?!%₀£$¢&#{[]}@©

ABCDEFGHIJKLMNOPQRSTUVWXYZ
abcdefghijklmnopqrstuvwxyz
1234567890 ..:;?!%₀£$¢&#{[]}@©

ABCDEFGHIJKLMNOPQRSTUVWXYZ
abcdefghijklmnopqrstuvwxyz
1234567890 ..:;?!%₀£$¢&#{[]}@©

DF Register Condensed

Bold Condensed
Bold Cond Italic

The quick brown fox jumps over the lazy dog.
THE QUICK BROWN FOX JUMPS OVER THE LAZY DOG.

The quick brown fox jumps over the lazy dog.
THE QUICK BROWN FOX JUMPS OVER THE LAZY DOG.

The quick brown fox jumps over the
THE QUICK BROWN FOX JUMPS OVER

ABCDEFGHIJKLMNOPQRSTUVWXYZ
abcdefghijklmnopqrstuvwxyz
1234567890 ,.:;?!%£$¢&#{[]}@©

ABCDEFGHIJKLMNOPQRSTUVWXYZ
abcdefghijklmnopqrstuvwxyz
1234567890 ,.:;?!%£$¢&#{[]}@©

DF Regulator A

Light
Light Italic
Bold
Bold Italic
Cameo

The quick brown fox jumps   ǧ alt ., & alt m, R alt 5, K ±, r alt =.
THE QUICK BROWN FOX JUMPS OVER THE LAZY DOG.

The quick brown fox jumps over the lazy dog.
THE QUICK BROWN FOX JUMPS OVER THE LAZY DOG

The quick brown fox jumps over the lazy d
THE QUICK BROWN FOX JUMPS OVER THE L

ABCDEFGHIJKLMNOPQRSTUVWXYZ
abcdefghijklmnopqrstuvwxyz
1234567890 ,.:;?!%£$¢&№{()}@©

ABCDEFGHIJKLMNOPQRSTUVWXYZ
abcdefghijklmnopqrstuvwxyz
1234567890 ,.:;?!%£$¢&№{()}@©

Light&**Bold**

Regulator Light and Regulator Bold 83pt

ABCDEFGHIJKLMNOPQRSTUVWXYZ
abcdefghijklmnopqrstuvwxyz
1234567890 ,.:;?!%£$¢&№{()}@©

ABCDEFGHIJKLMNOPQRSTUVWXYZ
abcdefghijklmnopqrstuvwxyz
1234567890 ,.;:?!%£$¢&ℕº{()}@©

ⒶⒷⒸⒹⒺⒻⒼⒽⒾⒿⓀⓁⓂⓃⓄⓅⓆⓇⓈⓉⓊⓋⓌⓍⓎⓏ
ⒶⒷⒸⒹⒺⒻⒼⒽⒾⒿⓀⓁⓂⓃⓄⓅⓆⓇⓈⓉⓊⓋⓌⓍⓎⓏ
①②③④⑤⑥⑦⑧⑨⓿● ● ● ● ? ! % £ $ ¢ & ℕº { (‹) }

DF Regulator B

Thin
Thin Italic
Medium
Medium Italic
Heavy
Heavy Italic

The quick brown fox jumps over the lazy dog
THE QUICK BROWN FOX JUMPS OVER THE LAZY DOG
The quick brown fox jumps over the lazy dog
THE QUICK BROWN FOX JUMPS OVER THE LAZY DOG
The quick brown fox jumps over the laz
THE QUICK BROWN FOX JUMPS OVER TH

ABCDEFGHIJKLMNOPQRSTUVWXYZ
abcdefghijklmnopqrstuvwxyz
1234567890 ,.;:?!%£$¢&ℕº{()}@©

ABCDEFGHIJKLMNOPQRSTUVWXYZ
abcdefghijklmnopqrstuvwxyz
1234567890 ,.;:?!%£$¢&ℕº{()}@©

Regulator Thin 72pt

ABCDEFGHIJKLMNOPQRSTUVWXYZ
abcdefghijklmnopqrstuvwxyz
1234567890 ,.;:?!%£$¢&ℕº{()}@©

ABCDEFGHIJKLMNOPQRSTUVWXYZ
abcdefghijklmnopqrstuvwxyz
1234567890 ,.;:?!%£$¢&ℕº{()}@©

ABCDEFGHIJKLMNOPQRSTUVWXYZ
abcdefghijklmnopqrstuvwxyz
1234567890 ,.;:?!%£$¢&№° {()} @©

ABCDEFGHIJKLMNOPQRSTUVWXYZ
abcdefghijklmnopqrstuvwxyz
1234567890 ,.;:?!%£$¢&№° {()} @©

DF Scrotnig

Medium
Medium Italic
Heavy
Heavy Italic
Condensed
Condensed Italic
Hexes One
Hexes Two

THE QUICK BROWN FOX JUMPS OVER THE LAZY DOG.
THE QUICK BROWN FOX JUMPS OVER THE LAZY DOG.

THE QUICK BROWN FOX JUMPS OVER THE LAZY D
THE QUICK BROWN FOX JUMPS OVER THE LAZY D

THE QUICK BROWN FOX JUMPS OVER
THE QUICK BROWN FOX JUMPS OVER

ABCDEFGHIJKLMNOPQRSTUVWXYZ
ABCDEFGHIJKLMNOPQRSTUVWXYZ
1234567890 ,.;:?!%£$(€)№ (()} @©

NEXT PROG

Scrotnig Medium 49pt

ABCDEFGHIJKLMNOPQRSTUVWXYZ
ABCDEFGHIJKLMNOPQRSTUVWXYZ
1234567890 ,.;:?!%£$(€)№ (()} @©

ABCDEFGHIJKLMNOPQRSTUVWXYZ
ABCDEFGHIJKLMNOPQRSTUVWXYZ
1234567890 ,.;:?!%£$(€)№ (()} @©

ABCDEFGHIJKLMNOPQRSTUVWXYZ
ABCDEFGHIJKLMNOPQRSTUVWXYZ
1234567890 ,.;:?!%£$(€)№ (()} @©

ABCDEFGHIJKLMNOPQRSTUVWXYZ
ABCDEFGHIJKLMNOPQRSTUVWXYZ
1234567890 ,.;:?!%£${€™(())}@©

ABCDEFGHIJKLMNOPQRSTUVWXYZ
ABCDEFGHIJKLMNOPQRSTUVWXYZ
1234567890 ,.;:?!%£${€™(())}@©

DF Silesia

Thin
Light
Medium
Bold
Heavy
Inline

The quick brown fox jumps over the lazy dog.
THE QUICK BROWN FOX JUMPS OVER THE LAZY DOG.

The quick brown fox jumps over the lazy dog.
THE QUICK BROWN FOX JUMPS OVER THE LA

The quick brown fox jumps over the lazy d
THE QUICK BROWN FOX JUMPS OVER

ABCDEFGHIJKLMNOPQRSTUVWXYZ
abcdefghijklmnopqrstuvwxyz
1234567890 ,.;:?!%£${€™+{[]}@©

ABCDEFGHIJKLMNOPQRSTUVWXYZ
abcdefghijklmnopqrstuvwxyz
1234567890 ,.;:?!%£${€™+{[]}@©

ABCDEFGHIJKLMNOPQRSTUVWXYZ
abcdefghijklmnopqrstuvwxyz
1234567890 ,.;:?!%£${€™+{[]}@©

ABCDEFGHIJKLMNOPQRSTUVWXYZ
abcdefghijklmnopqrstuvwxyz
1234567890 ,.:;?!%2&$+÷{[]}@©

ABCDEFGHIJKLMNOPQRSTUVWXYZ
abcdefghijklmnopqrstuvwxyz
1234567890 ,.:;?!%2&$+÷{[]}@©

ABCDEFGHIJKLMNOPQRSTUVWXYZ
abcdefghijklmnopqrstuvwxyz
1234567890 ,.:;?!%2&$+÷{[]}@©

DF Sinclair

Biform
Display

The quick brown fox jumps over the lazy dog.
THE QUICK BROWN FOX JUMPS OVER THE LAZY DOG.

The quick brown fox jumps over the lazy dog.
THE QUICK BROWN FOX JUMPS OVER THE LAZY DOG.

The quick brown fox jumps over the lazy dog.
THE QUICK BROWN FOX JUMPS OVER THE LAZY DOG.

ABCDEFGHIJKLMNOPQRSTUVWXYZ abcdefghijklmno
pqrstuvwxyz 1234567890 ,.;:?!%£$(&!K{()}@©

ABCDEFGHIJKLMNOPQRSTUVWXYZ abcdefghijklmno
pqrstuvwxyz 1234567890 ,.;:?!%£$(&!K{()}@©

DF Skylab

Regular
Capsule
Code

THE QUICK BROWN FOX JUMPS OVER THE LAZY DOG.
THE QUICK BROWN FOX JUMPS OVER THE LAZY DOG.

THE QUICK BROWN FOX JUMPS OVER THE LAZY DOG.
THE QUICK BROWN FOX JUMPS OVER THE LAZY DOG.

THE QUICK BROWN FOX JUMPS OVER THE
THE QUICK BROWN FOX JUMPS OVER THE

ABCDEFGHIJKLMNOPQRSTUVWXYZ
ABCDEFGHIJKLMNOPQRSTUVWXYZ
1234567890 ,.:;?!%£$&+{()} @©

SOLARIS

Skylab Regular 69pt

DF Slack Casual

Medium
Medium Italic
Bold
Bold Italic

[Ea]

The quick brown Fox jumps over the lazy dog.
THE QUICK BROWN FOX JUMPS OVER THE LAZY DOG.

The quick brown Fox jumps over the lazy dog.
THE QUICK BROWN FOX JUMPS OVER THE LAZY DOG.

The quick brown Fox jumps over the lazy dog.
THE QUICK BROWN FOX JUMPS OVER THE LAZY DOG.

ABCDEFGHIJKLMNOPQRSTUVWXYZ abcdefghijklmnopqrstu
vwxyz 1234567890 .,:;?!%0£$¢&#{[]}@©

ABCDEFGHIJKLMNOPQRSTUVWXYZ abcdefghijklmnopqrstu
vwxyz 1234567890 .,:;?!%0£$¢&#{[]}@©

ABCDEFGHIJKLMNOPQRSTUVWXYZ abcdefghijklmnopqrstu
vwxyz 1234567890 .,:;?!%0£$¢&#{[]}@©

ABCDEFGHIJKLMNOPQRSTUVWXYZ abcdefghijklmnopqrstu
vwxyz 1234567890 .,:;?!%0£$¢&#{[]}@©

DF Space Cadet

Regular

THE QUICK BROWN FOX JUMPS OVER THE LAZY DOG.
THE QUICK BROWN FOX JUMPS OVER THE LAZY DOG.

THE QUICK BROWN FOX JUMPS OVER THE LAZY DOG.
THE QUICK BROWN FOX JUMPS OVER THE LAZY DOG.

THE QUICK BROWN FOX JUMPS OVER THE
THE QUICK BROWN FOX JUMPS OVER THE

ABCDEFGHIJKLMNOPQRSTUVWXYZ
1234567890 .,:;?!%£$¢&#-[()]@©

DF Stadia

Regular
Outline

The quick brown fox jumps over the lazy dog.
THE QUICK BROWN FOX JUMPS OVER THE LAZY DOG.

The quick brown fox jumps over the lazy dog.
THE QUICK BROWN FOX JUMPS OVER THE LAZY DOG.

The quick brown fox jumps over the
THE QUICK BROWN FOX JUMPS OVER THE

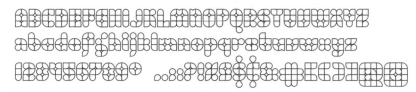

Stadia
Regular 87pt

DF Substation

Regular

THE QUICK BROWN FOX JUMPS OVER THE LAZY DOG.
THE QUICK BROWN FOX JUMPS OVER THE LAZY DOG.

THE QUICK BROWN FOX JUMPS OVER THE LAZY DOG.
THE QUICK BROWN FOX JUMPS OVER THE LAZY DOG.

THE QUICK BROWN FOX JUMPS OVER
THE QUICK BROWN FOX JUMPS OVER

ABCDEFGHIJKLMNOPQRSTUVWXYZ
ABCDEFGHIJKLMNOPQRSTUVWXYZ
1234567890 .,:;?!%£$¢&#(()]@©

DF Telecast

Regular
Spare Parts

THE QUICK BROWN FOX JUMPS OVER THE LAZY DOG.
THE QUICK BROWN FOX JUMPS OVER THE LAZY DOG.

THE QUICK BROWN FOX JUMPS OVER THE LAZY DOG.
THE QUICK BROWN FOX JUMPS OVER THE LAZY DOG.

THE QUICK BROWN FOX JUMPS OVER THE LA
THE QUICK BROWN FOX JUMPS OVER THE LA

ABCDEFGHIJKLMNOPQRSTUVWXYZ
ABCDEFGHIJKLMNOPQRSTUVWXYZ
1234567890 ,.:;?!%£$¢&#(){}@©

CATHODE SCANNER

Use 'Spare Parts' at the
start and end of words

DF Terrazzo

Regular

ABCDEFGHIJKLMNOPQRSTUVWXYZ
ABCDEFGHIJKLMNOPQRSTUVWXYZ
1234567890

DF Transmat

Regular
Terminals

THE QUICK BROWN FOX JUMPS OVER THE LAZY DOG.
THE QUICK BROWN FOX JUMPS OVER THE LAZY DOG.

THE QUICK BROWN FOX JUMPS OVER THE LAZY DOG.
THE QUICK BROWN FOX JUMPS OVER THE LAZY DOG.

THE QUICK BROWN FOX JUMPS OVER THE L
THE QUICK BROWN FOX JUMPS OVER THE L

ABCDEFGHIJKLMNOPQRSTUVWXYZ
ABCDEFGHIJKLMNOPQRSTUVWXYZ
1234567890

CATHODE SCANNER

Use 'Terminals' at the
start and end of words

DF Untitled 1

Regular

→ alt 5, ↓ alt ., ↑ alt ,, Tᴇ|· alt m, ꜰ☐x alt d, ᴛʜ☐ alt w,
☐ꜰ shift alt p, ʏ! alt p, ɪɴ alt z, ☐ alt l, ☐ alt v, ☐ alt j.

THE QUICK BROWN FOX JUMPS OVER THE LAZY DOG.
THE QUICK BROWN FOX JUMPS OVER THE LAZY DOG.

THE QUICK BROWN FOX JUMPS OVER
THE QUICK BROWN FOX JUMPS OVER T

ABCDEFGHIJKLMNOPQRSTUVWXYZ
ABCDEFGHIJKLMNOPQRSTUVWXYZ
1234567890 ,.;:?!%o£$¢&NO{[]}@©

DF Vertex

Light
Medium
Demi Bold
Bold
Inline

The quick brown fox jumps over the lazy dog.
THE QUICK BROWN FOX JUMPS OVER THE LAZY DOG.

8 alt 5

The quick brown fox jumps over the lazy dog.
THE QUICK BROWN FOX JUMPS OVER THE LAZY DOG.

The quick brown fox jumps over
THE QUICK BROWN FOX JUMPS OVE

ABCDEFGHIJKLMNOPQRSTUVWXYZ
abcdefghijklmnopqrstuvwxyz
1234567890 ,_;:?!%€$¢&#{()}@©

ABCDEFGHIJKLMNOPQRSTUVWXYZ
abcdefghijklmnopqrstuvwxyz
1234567890 ,_;:?!%€$¢&#{()}@©

ABCDEFGHIJKLMNOPQRSTUVWXYZ
abcdefghijklmnopqrstuvwxyz
1234567890 ,_;:?!%€$¢&#{()}@©

ABCDEFGHIJKLMNOPQRSTUVWXYZ
abcdefghijklmnopqrstuvwxyz
1234567890 ,_;:?!%€$¢&#{()}@©

ABCDEFGHIJKLMNOPQRSTUVWXYZ
abcdefghijklmnopqrstuvwxyz
1234567890 ,_;:?!%€$¢&#{()}@©

DF Westway

Eastbound
Westbound

THE QUICK BROWN FOX JUMPS OVER THE LAZY DOG.
THE QUICK BROWN FOX JUMPS OVER THE LAZY DOG.

THE QUICK BROWN FOX JUMPS OVER THE LAZY DOG.
THE QUICK BROWN FOX JUMPS OVER THE LAZY DOG.

THE QUICK BROWN FOX JUMPS OVER
THE QUICK BROWN FOX JUMPS OVER

ABCDEFGHIJKLMNOPQRSTUVWXYZ
ABCDEFGHIJKLMNOPQRSTUVWXYZ
1234567890 ,.;:?!%£$¢#()@©

ABCDEFGHIJKLMNOPQRSTUVWXYZ
ABCDEFGHIJKLMNOPQRSTUVWXYZ
1234567890 ,.;:?!%£$¢#()@©

DF Wexford Oakley

Regular
Alternates

The quick brown fox jumps over the lazy dog.
THE QUICK BROWN FOX JUMPS OVER THE LAZY DOG.

The quick brown fox jumps over the lazy dog.
THE QUICK BROWN FOX JUMPS OVER THE LAZY DOG

The quick brown fox jumps over the la
THE QUICK BROWN FOX JUMPS OVE

ABCDEFGHIJKLMNOPQRSTUVWXYZ
abcdefghijklmnopqrstuvwxyz
1234567890 ,.;:?!%£$¢&#{()}@©

ABCDEFGHIJKLMNOPQRSTUVWXYZ
abcdefghijklmnopqrstuvwxyz
1234567890 ,.;:?!%£$¢&#{()}@©

DF WhyTwoKay

Regular

DF Zinger

Regular
Italic

The quick brown fox jumps over the lazy d
THE QUICK BROWN FOX JUMPS OVER THE LAZY D

The quick brown fo
THE QUICK BROWN FO

The quick br
THE QUICK BR

ABCDEFGHIJKLMNOPQ
RSTUVWXYZabcdefgh
ijklmnopqrstuvwxyz
1234567890
. , ; : ? ! % £ $ ¢ & # @ ©

ABCDEFGHIJKLMNOPQ
RSTUVWXYZabcdefgh
ijklmnopqrstuvwxyz
1234567890
. , ; : ? ! % £ $ ¢ & # @ ©

zap

Zinger Italic 71pt

Alphabetical Index

Miserichordia Regular 60pt

"How can there be too many
typefaces in the world?
Are there too many songs,
too many books, too many new
places to go?"